D1557998

THE
QUALITY
ROADMAP

THE
QUALITY
ROADMAP

How to Get Your Company on the Quality Track– And Keep It There

Ray Svenson   Karen Wallace
Guy Wallace   Bruce Wexler

amacom
AMERICAN MANAGEMENT ASSOCIATION

New York • Atlanta • Boston • Chicago • Kansas City • San Francisco • Washington, D.C.
Brussels • Mexico City • Tokyo • Toronto

This book is available at a special
discount when ordered in bulk quantities.
For information, contact Special Sales Department,
AMACOM, a division of American Management Association,
135 West 50th Street, New York, NY 10020.

This publication is designed to provide accurate and authoritative
information in regard to the subject matter covered. It is sold with
the understanding that the publisher is not engaged in rendering
legal, accounting, or other professional service. If legal advice or
other expert assistance is required, the services of a competent
professional person should be sought.

AMACOM Books, a division of American Management Association
135 West 50th Street, New York, NY 10020

This book is also distributed by: Quality Resources
A division of The Kraus Organization, Ltd.
One Water Street, White Plains, New York 10601
ISBN 0-527-76245-8

Library of Congress Cataloging-in-Publication Data

The Quality roadmap : how to get your company on the quality track—
    and keep it there / Ray Svenson, Karen Wallace, Guy Wallace, with
    Bruce Wexler.
        p.   cm.
    Includes index.
    ISBN 0-8144-5117-9
    1. Total quality management.   I. Svenson, Raynold A.
II. Wallace, Karen, 1945–   .   III. Wallace, Guy.   IV. Title:
Quality road map.
HD62.15.Q364   1994
658.5'62—dc20   93-31608
                                                                CIP

Printing number

10   9   8   7   6   5   4   3   2   1

To all the Gurus . . .

. . . those quality and human performance technology pioneers who went first and collectively charted the wilderness.

Contents

Forewords

By Pete Hamm, President/CEO, Council for Continuous Improvement

Change is a constant in business. To respond to the dynamics of change, businesses must maximize their efficiency and effectiveness. One of the best ways to do so is to learn what works for others—as well as what doesn't work. Facilitating this learning process was the impetus for the Council for Continuous Improvement (CCI).

Our group was incorporated in 1990 as a nonprofit consortium of companies with the mission to share and document our experiences with quality and continuous improvement programs. In three years, our membership has dramatically increased by 200 percent. Our members represent a diverse group of interests, including manufacturing, service, academia, and government.

While the relatively informal learning exchange we created was beneficial, it wasn't sufficient. We required a process, a disciplined methodology that would enable us to answer questions such as: Where are we? Where do we want to go? How do we get there?

We needed a roadmap.

As president/CEO of CCI, I was charged with responding to this need. I helped form a focus group to develop a system—a roadmap—for our members to follow in their pursuit of continuous improvement. The map was intended to be comprehensive, addressing improvement issues in all aspects of the business and at all levels.

To assist us in reaching this ambitious objective of developing a roadmap, we established a partnership with Svenson & Wallace, a consulting firm that had done extensive work for clients in process improvement areas.

After much effort, we finally produced an innovative and effective roadmap that we're now making available to our members. This book also makes it available to *you*. As you'll discover, *The Quality Roadmap* not only starts you on the road to continuous improvement, but it helps you get back on track if you somehow become lost. At a time when many organizations are struggling with TQM and improvement issues, this is truly a timely and valuable book.

By Mark Graham Brown

Companies just getting started on a journey toward Total Quality Management are very confused. There is an overwhelming amount of information on different aspects and approaches for improving quality and customer satisfaction. There are more than 100 different books on the market that address the topic, at least six regular periodicals on Total Quality, and thousands of consultants who are ready to help you on your journey. The hardest part of Total Quality today is trying to figure out whom to listen to and which approach to select.

It's hard to find a company that is not working on implementing Total Quality. Some have become interested in TQM out of desperation. Companies that have had a near-death experience have found that it is very easy to get everyone in the organization committed to a major change effort—they're all living in fear of losing their jobs. Others have become involved because their major customers demanded that they have a quality program or effort in place if they want to keep the customers' business. Motorola received a lot of press for requiring all of its suppliers to apply for the Malcolm Baldrige National Quality Award. A minority of companies that are not experiencing problems today are working on implementing Total Quality to stay one step ahead of the competition and ensure their future success. These companies have a harder time making the major systems changes needed to take Total Quality from being a program to being integrated into day-to-day business operations.

Integration is really what this book is all about. We're told that TQM is not a program, it is a way of managing an organization. Yet, just the fact that it has a name that can be abbreviated with three initials tells most employees that it is nothing more than another program. TQM sounds and looks like SPC, MBO, JIT, ABC, and any of the other "three-initial" programs companies have embarked on in the last fifteen years. One of the most difficult aspects of TQM is taking it from being a program to being the standard way a company operates. It's easy to do this in a start-up operation. AT&T's Universal Card Systems, formed in

1989, used the Baldrige Award criteria as a foundation for creating all its systems. Federal Express, another Baldrige Award winner, has never had a quality "program." The company has always been run by using the principles of TQM. But how do you change the culture of a 100-year-old company with 20,000 employees that has a management style and systems that are very contrary to the tenets of TQM? This is part of what you will learn in this book.

What makes this book unique in comparison to the hundred or so other books on the market addressing TQM is that it provides a map to help you plan and negotiate your route toward becoming a Total Quality culture. What you can currently find out there are cookbooks, general guidelines, and theory. Hence, the need for a book like this. This is not a cookbook. It does not provide you with a series of checklists that if followed will provide you with a TQM organization. It is also not a theory book or a set of general guidelines. It really is a map. A map does not give you directions or tell you the best route to take. It provides you with an understanding of all the different routes that you can take to get to various destinations. This book provides you with a way to make sense out of all the different quality-related tools, concepts, and approaches. It fits with whatever quality guru you happen to follow; it also fits if you follow none of them.

Most of the press reports you read today concerning Total Quality talk about how it doesn't work. A couple of recent headlines from the *Wall Street Journal* proclaim:

"Quality Programs Show Shoddy Results"
"Baldrige Award Losing Luster"

If Total Quality is such an outstanding way of improving an organization's performance, why is it that about two-thirds of the companies that try it end up failing or dropping the effort? For every study that says it works, there is another study that says it doesn't. For every story about how TQM saved a company from going under and changed its culture, there are other stories about how this approach does not guarantee business success. The Wallace Company, a Baldrige winner, filed for bankruptcy in 1992, and AT&T's plant that won the Baldrige Award in 1992 announced it was having a major layoff in May 1993.

Total Quality Management is an effective way of improving a company's performance and ensuring its long-term survival. However, there are no guarantees. The major reason that TQM fails in many companies is not that the companies are inherently defective. The major reason is that the companies have not figured out how to integrate TQM into their overall business strategy and management systems, and how to tailor the approach to fit their company. Both of these issues are addressed in this book. I think that this book will be of great help to companies that are just beginning the quality journey, or have begun the journey and gotten lost on the way.

Acknowledgments

The authors wish to acknowledge Edward Jones, Jones, Reilly & Associates, Inc., and the CCI Architecture Special Interest Group, all of whom contributed materially to the roadmap concept and details; our clients, who have provided the experience basis; Frank Mallinder for his presentation suggestions; and the SWI staff for steadfast graphics and production support.

Introduction

Why are so many companies floundering as they attempt to implement quality programs? Why have the great expectations engendered by TQM not been met?

We've asked ourselves these questions more than once. We know of scores of organizations that have tried and failed to make their quality efforts work. We've listened to Baldrige Award people declare that it would take ten years for companies to get systems in place that would make them viable award candidates.

Something was wrong. As human performance technologists (HPTs), we knew there had to be a way to reach quality goals faster, cheaper, and better. As a consulting firm working with clients struggling with TQM, we had a good business reason to come up with a way to do so.

As we began working on this issue, we made three fascinating discoveries. First, we found that American companies' attempts to mimic the Total Quality Management (TQM) approach of the Japanese were premature. The Japanese have been practicing TQM (actually, they refer to it as Total Quality Control) for years. They now have the luxury of improving relatively minor processes throughout the organization because they have already met major improvement targets. American organizations, in the early stages of quality efforts, don't have that luxury. Yet we still try to improve everything, large and small, at once— we spend millions of dollars to train an entire work force and set up hundreds of improvement teams. As a result, we spread our resources too thin, and the results are disappointing, accounting for much of the frustration with the quality movement. The opposite approach seemed to make more sense: to focus our resources on specific improvement targets that would yield significant business results. Such an approach would demonstrate the value of TQM and build excitement and momentum for it throughout the organization. But we found relatively few organizations employing this targeted methodology.

Second, our efforts led us to the conclusion that there was a lack of knowledge about or a prejudice against human performance technology (HPT), a discipline that would be of great value to quality aspirants. Part of the problem was that the quality movement's roots are in manufacturing and our initial response to the Japanese challenge was rooted there as well. As a result, the gurus who supported the Japanese quality revolution, like Deming and Juran, have become well known, whereas HPT gurus, like Gilbert, Rummler, and Mager, have not.

Third, we realized that many organizations seemed to be pursuing quality for quality's sake. Companies were using quality tools and principles with scant consideration for business strategy or goals, or at least with no clear link between them. It was as if a quality effort would automatically yield business gains. Not only was that not the case, but in some instances, quality efforts actually caused business losses. It was all too easy for a company to improve low-impact processes or for an improved process to throw related processes out of whack. Unless there was a concerted effort from the beginning to integrate business strategy with process improvements, the odds were that a quality effort would have no discernible impact on the ultimate metric for a held business: growth of shareholder value.

With these three points in mind, we created the roadmap that will be explained in this book. As you'll see, the roadmap is not a one-dimensional set of directions that leads toward quality. Instead, it is a three-dimensional cube that provides you with a planning and management framework for getting there. This framework enables you to juxtapose where you are now (with your quality effort) against the ideal. When you see the gaps that exist, you understand what you have to do to close them.

Neither the roadmap nor this book makes quality easy. No book or tool can. What they do do is give you what you've been missing: an effective planning guide for implementing quality. Most books assume you've already done your planning or that you'll naturally do so effectively; they provide tools and techniques (many of which are quite good). But without a sound business approach to quality, these tools and techniques are useless. In this book, you'll find an approach that enables you to do the following:

- Start your quality program off on the right road by pinpointing the areas of improvement that will yield the most significant results for your business.
- Plan your quality effort not just for the next few months, but for

the next few years, setting up a series of improvement targets that are in the right strategic order.
- Take the frustration out of TQM by giving you greater control of where your quality effort is going and helping you to get there faster, more cheaply, and more effectively.

Underlying the roadmap is our experience with and belief in HPT. It's not a concept that we recently came upon or just started exploring. For many years, it has been the guiding principle behind our consulting firm's work. We'd like to explain briefly what HPT is and how our backgrounds with performance technology led to the roadmap concept.

The military developed performance technology during World War II when it needed a quick way to train people to perform complex tasks such as building bombs. Assembling cross-discipline teams of psychologists, educators, and other specialists, it created the foundation of performance technology. Later, students of famed behavioral psychologist B. F. Skinner attempted to apply lessons from their approach in combination with performance technology in work settings. Ultimately, HPT evolved into an eclectic but cohesive blend of behavioral psychology, systems engineering, and measurement theory.

One of the HPT gurus, Tom Gilbert, described it as "the conversion of human potential into human capital." Another definition is: "A systems approach to analyze organizational and individual performance and redesign to improve that performance." Still another: "A powerful collection of theories and methods that enables systematic maximization of organization performance." Whatever the definition, the key words are *human, performance,* and *systematic.*

Of the three authors of this book, Karen Wallace was the first one to come across HPT when she was working as a training manager for Blue Cross/Blue Shield in Michigan. We'll let Karen relate her initial experience with performance technology:

> I was introduced to HPT through a workshop I attended given by Praxis Corp., a company owned by HPT leaders Tom Gilbert and Geary Rummler. In 1975, I was charged with "re-engineering" a department that handled recovery of funds for the insurance company. Using HPT for the first time, I improved the performance of the department from recovery of $6 million to recovery of $12 million annually. Without increasing expenditures by one penny, we doubled our recovery, and that $6 million fell directly to the bottom line.

Performance technology made perfect sense to me as a trainer. I had conducted training sessions in which people learned to do certain things a certain way, and yet the training turned out to be inadequate because their performance eventually declined. I couldn't figure out what I had done wrong, why I had to retrain them. Something was missing, and that something turned out to be answered by performance technology.

Karen's performance technology expertise dovetailed with the skills of Ray Svenson and Guy Wallace. Ray had experience as a systems engineer and as a long-range and technology planner at Bell Labs and AT&T. Guy came out of Motorola and had been involved in training and project management. When we joined forces in 1981, we all subscribed to performance technology principles, but we had three additional core competencies: systems engineering, planning, and project management. As the quality movement gained steam and our clients requested our help on specific projects, we started integrating TQM and HPT. Initially, we were called in to help make improvements at a process or departmental level. But when companies started asking us for a top-down approach—a way to revamp a company from the executive level on down in a quest for quality—we recognized that we had to create a new framework: the roadmap. Working with clients as diverse as engineering departments, manufacturers, accounting firms, and oil-field operators, we put aspects of the roadmap into use. Though we'll discuss the roadmap's evolution in greater detail in later chapters, the important point here is that it effectively addressed quality movement issues using HPT concepts.

TQM and HPT share many principles and techniques. Both focus on measured improvement, though TQM makes greater use of statistical tools than HPT. The process mapping tool in HPT translates into TQM's flowcharting, for instance. HPT's management by objectives becomes policy deployment in TQM.

Despite these parallels, the TQM movement has not capitalized on HPT—at least, not to the extent that it should. While a few quality gurus may acknowledge the usefulness of some of performance technology's tools, most overlook them, even as organizations desperately search for ways to deal with the relatively softer issues such as planning, system design, motivation, training, teamwork, and system integration.

We believe that many of the problems that beset TQM-candidate companies can be solved through our HPT-inspired roadmap. We've found that it can be effective no matter what your business is or the size of your organization. We've learned that the roadmap is flexible enough to adapt to any viable quality theory. We've seen it work for companies that are just starting out with quality and for those that have been at it a while and have gotten stuck.

It's not a panacea. But until one comes along, it's the best guide we've found for an organization's quality journey.

Chapter 1

Total Quality vs. Partial Quality

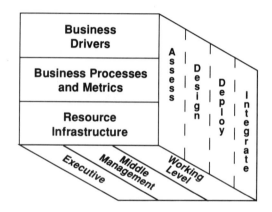

The United States is in the midst of a major paradigm shift from mass production to lean production. It is as monumental a shift as the one that occurred during the Industrial Revolution when we evolved from a craft production mode to one of mass production. The way we manage, market, and manufacture—the way we run all aspects of our business—will be dramatically different sooner than most people think.

Every organization must come to terms with the new paradigm. Every company must make the transition from the hierarchical, segregated functions of the past to the flattened structure and cross-functional teams of the future. We use the word *must* because the transition will not be a matter of choice. Any company that wants to be productive, competitive, and profitable in the future will have to change. And any company that glimpses the future will want to change—numerous exciting opportunities will exist for organizations that have made the transition to the new paradigm.

Though it's not an easy transition, a tool does exist to facilitate it. This tool is called Total Quality Management (TQM). As you probably know, there has been a great deal of discussion and debate over what TQM really is and if it really works. Before providing what we feel is a viable definition of TQM, here's a synopsis of the quality movement's evolution and why its efficacy has been called into question.

A Brief History of "Quality" and Its Many Manifestations

In the beginning, there was the quality defect inspection phase. Product-focused, this early quality initiative moved from 100 percent final inspection to statistical sampling of products to spot defective lots. From there, we evolved to a proactive stance: We began controlling the key variables of the production process to avoid rather than to catch defects. The next stage was to design the product robustly so that it was easier to produce, use, and maintain—in other words, we designed out potential defects before they occurred. Finally, we made it to the current phase, in which approaches to the management of quality impact all business processes, not just manufacturing—in other words, total quality.

Long after the Japanese embraced W. Edwards Deming's quality principles and put them to good use, the Naval Systems Air Commands coined the term *Total Quality Management* in 1985 to describe its Japanese-style management approach to quality improvement. A few years later, the General Accounting Office reported to Congress about Malcolm Baldrige Award winners and detailed how TQM generally led to corporate performance improvements in market share, customer satisfaction, employee relations, productivity, and profitability.

At that point, many companies jumped on the bandwagon. It's hard to find a major corporation that hasn't launched some type of quality effort. Unfortunately, many of those companies have been disappointed—the miracle promised by the quality gurus didn't come to pass. Frustrated and unhappy, many erstwhile quality supporters spoke out against the TQM movement, claiming it promised more than it delivered.

But the problem went deeper than that. TQM became so big so fast that it spawned a multiplicity of gurus, definitions, and labels. These overlapping and gapped concepts and precepts have led to much confusion. Today, even the term *quality* has so many meanings that it has become almost useless. Here are three sample definitions of quality that have emerged:

"Quality is meeting the requirements of customers, both inside and outside the organization, for defect-free products, services, and business processes."—IBM

"Quality is the ability of a product or service to meet the expectations of customers."—AT&T Process Quality Guidelines

"Improvement of the process increases uniformity of output of product, reduces rework and mistakes, reduces waste of manpower, machine-time, and materials, and thus increases output with less effort."—W. Edwards Deming

Along with these and many other definitions came numerous labels for the overall movement: TQC (Total Quality Control), the more prevalent Japanese term; TQS (Total Quality Success); TQI (Total Quality Improvement); CQI (Continuous Quality Improvement); CI (Continuous Improvement); TQL (Total Quality Leadership). The list goes on.

Confusion was inevitable. Some companies attempted to combine elements of the old mass production paradigm with elements of TQM, not realizing that they were mixing oil and water. Again, we don't blame those companies. Without a universally accepted definition of TQM, such a mixture was to be expected. Unfortunately, such a definition is difficult to articulate. One of the most revealing aspects of the GAO report on Baldrige Award winners was that each winner had developed its own unique approach to TQM. As a result, each organization has its own definition based on that approach.

But it's possible to define TQM within parameters broader than a sentence or two. This book and the roadmap it describes do just that.

Is your organization pursuing TQM from a holistic perspective? Or is it taking a narrower point of view? If the latter, you may find yourself thinking TQM but inadvertently doing PQM—partial quality management. As the name implies, PQM is a partial approach to quality; some essential ingredients are missing. The following examples will give you a sense of some of PQM's common manifestations and how they miss the mark.

Examples of Partial Quality Management

• *High concept, low implementation.* The quality effort starts with a bang. Top management goes about the quality education process with missionary zeal. Meetings are held, gurus are brought in to preach, signs are posted, training sessions are provided, teams are created. But after the initial indoctrination period, enthusiasm and energy wane. Management has failed to set improvement targets; newly created teams at lower levels are working on improvements virtually at random. Executive leadership loses interest in quality efforts, especially when they fail to meet expectations. While top management's commitment to quality may have been total at the start, this commitment slips from total to partial after that initial burst of enthusiasm.

• *Manufacturing only.* Because the impetus for quality often comes from the manufacturing area, the emphasis often remains there. Many organizations focus on production processes to the exclusion of all else, viewing quality as something confined to the factory floor. But even if the primary goal is related to product quality, that goal won't be achieved unless other processes are brought into the strategy. Too often, sales, information management, finance, and customer service groups are cut off from the quality initiative. The organization is unsure of how to make the transition off the production floor and into the remaining processes of the business. Failure to move elsewhere ensures PQM.

• *Limited resources.* Total quality commitments from management aren't only verbal (walking the talk); they must also involve the deployment of time, money, and people. More than one CEO has pulled the plug on a quality strategy because it didn't provide an ROI fast enough. There's no such thing as instant quality. Though TQM can yield some incremental gains fairly quickly, major progress usually comes after the first two years. Setting arbitrary or unrealistic deadlines is PQM at its worst. The same is true of failing to provide adequate direction and resources for teams striving to make improvements. Sometimes, the up-front investment in quality can be expensive—you may have to build a new plant, create a new material, or redesign your information systems. But it's more expensive to go the PQM route, since under-resourced improvements go nowhere or worse. Finally, management must staff improvement teams with the right people. If management withholds these people under the assumption that "they can't be spared because they're too important to the business," PQM happens. Nothing is more important to the business than making the transition to quality. If the best people aren't on your improvement teams, you won't get the best results.

• *Separate and unequal.* Creating a quality effort separate from or parallel to the effort to "run the business" is inimical to TQM. Though the intentions may be good (a separate group is freed from the mundane details and politics of day-to-day business), the results are often poor. If a group is outside the mainstream, its members are viewed as outsiders. Running the business will always come first, and quality improvement will come second. Separate quality teams frequently have too little clout and are often perceived as temporary. To avoid this type of PQM, integrate quality teams and efforts into the running of the business.

• *Philosophy without structure.* One of the most common examples of PQM, this involves an effort that has very strong, motivating quality principles but relatively weak implementation strategy and tactics. Many times, we've seen organizations embark on quality journeys with much sound and fury—they do a brilliant job of espousing the principles of a quality guru and generate tremendous excitement about what quality will mean to the organization. But after the initial excitement subsides, there's no plan or capability to fulfill the quality promise. The resources aren't there, the company hasn't been properly organized into teams, a direction is lacking, and so on. Once, we walked into a company that had posters on the wall that read, "Do it right the first time." But the company hadn't given its employees any of the tools to do it right at any time. Please don't misunderstand our point. Philosophical leadership is just as important as structural leadership. You need the hype, the excitement, that the posters, speeches, and motivational sessions provide. But there has to be an appropriate balance between philosophy and structure. If that balance is absent, PQM occurs.

A Double-Edged Sword

Don't berate yourself or feel that all is lost if any of these PQM examples hit close to home. We've found that PQM doesn't have to be the frustrating end point it seems to be—that PQM can be a stepping stone to a successful TQM program. Because TQM is often an overwhelming, complex concept, it helps to gain many experiences with it—even some negative experiences can be worthwhile to a "learning organization." Lessons learned about what not to do often make it easier to do the right thing first, next time.

One of the ways to learn from PQM is not to be deceived by it. PQM can easily masquerade as TQM. A partial quality effort can make things happen; it can get your organization to the point of establishing empowered teams, and perhaps getting positive results.

But they may not be sustainable results.

Or you may not be able to deploy a successful improvement in other areas of the company.

Or the effort may lead you just so far and no farther—you find yourself at a dead end with no idea of how to continue your quality efforts elsewhere.

TQM, unlike PQM, has no inherently limiting or segregating elements. It's integrated with all aspects of the leadership, management, and work efforts of the business. A lack of integration is a dead giveaway that PQM is operative. For instance, when a company holds a meeting about quality, there are generally items on the agenda such as: How are we progressing in terms of empowering our people? How are our improvements in the sales process going? Is our training curriculum in place and what's going to be the next course offered? After the meeting, everyone goes off to work on his or her particular action items. There's no coordination in finding answers to the questions. The people in training are buried in the infrastructure, and they're not coordinating their efforts with the people who are working on sales process improvements.

Also, a lack of clear priorities for targeted improvements signals a PQM effort. If newly trained and empowered teams are not initially directed by management, each team will work on those quality issues it readily sees. Thus, water cooler issues are addressed, or a partial process is suboptimized.

The result: quality for quality's sake, rather than for the business's sake.

PQM ignores the larger business goal, strategy, or framework. Improvement actions are taken to satisfy a quality principle or training imperative. There's no connection to business results. *As wonderful as quality principles such as empowerment and teamwork are, they're means to an end, not the end themselves.* TQM demands that any type of training program or improvement be driven by specific business needs, not by some vague quality construct.

Understanding the difference between TQM and PQM is crucial. Significantly, companies that have been PQM practitioners tend to understand the difference better than those that are coming to the quality movement without any experience. It's almost as if you have to know what the wrong road to TQM is before you can recognize the right one.

Given that recognition, the next step is to get started without getting lost. A roadmap will help you move in the right direction.

A Map to Make Sense of Where We've Been, Where We Are, and Where We're Going

Given the prevalence of PQM, the lack of a universal definition for TQM, and the general confusion that surrounds the continuously evolving quality movement, we need a logical, complete, sequential approach to implementing TQM and making quality work. Without this approach, it's too easy to make mistakes. We may deploy quality concepts, tools, and techniques, but we won't achieve the desired effect on the business. Without strategic control in your approach, your quality efforts will be all over the map.

Most organizations don't even realize such a map exists. Rather than going in ten different directions at once, you can coordinate and chart your organization's efforts with a quality roadmap. Based on performance improvement work with our clients over many years, we've created such a map. How this map evolved and how you can use it will be discussed in detail in Chapter 2. For now, we'd simply like to convince you that a map is both desirable and necessary.

Quality is inherently complex. Anyone who tries to sell a quick and easy solution to quality improvement is selling you a load of very poor quality stuff. Because of this complexity, companies can easily get lost or disoriented or become impatient on their way to achieving their quality goals. Here are some questions that frequently arise on the journey and that cause organizations to take the wrong paths or become roadblocked:

- How do we know that all the teams we've set up are doing useful work?
- How can we justify the high cost of all the quality training we're doing?
- What are we going to do with all our middle managers who don't seem to have a place in the new, lean production paradigm?
- It's been over a year since we launched the program and our bottom line isn't any better than it was before; how do we measure if we're making progress?
- Is there some way we can control the benefit-to-cost ratio, or do we simply have to take all this on faith?
- How do we sell an improvement created in one plant to all the other plants; how do we overcome the natural resistance to an improvement that was "invented" somewhere else?
- How can we sell this to the board of directors?
- The union hates the word *quality*, since it translates (to them) into loss of jobs; how can we sell them on quality?
- What can executive leadership do to focus the effort and accelerate results?
- How do we break down the barriers between functional groups and get them to work productively in cross-functional teams?

These and similar questions confound and confuse management. It's tempting to junk the quality initiative rather than deal with an angry union or retrain/redeploy hundreds of middle managers. In our confusion, we may even do the wrong thing rather than nothing—instead of avoiding the middle management issue, we arbitrarily cut out a layer and terminate all of them, ensuring plunging employee morale and growing fear that will destroy any attempt to implement a quality improvement strategy.

Our map gives us a way to answer these questions with a certain degree of assurance. It allows us to study the entire landscape, revealing all the possible paths and choosing the ones with the best return on investment. Exhibit 1-1 is a preview.

As you can see, this does not resemble a traditional map in any way—its basic geometric unit is a three-sided cube. For the moment, ignore the bottom and side of the cube and focus on the front face, the one that contains *business drivers, business processes and metrics,* and *resource infrastructure.* Those three segments are further broken down into component parts. Business drivers drive the definition of required business processes and metrics, and the processes and metrics in turn drive the definition of the required resources in the infrastructure. But beware: The process is iterative and not linear.

Our cube roadmap is nothing new or mysterious. As we noted in our introduction, it embodies principles not only of TQM, but of human performance technology (HPT). Combining the tools, techniques, and motivation of HPT with the philosophies, concepts, and statistical overlay of TQM, the roadmap will help you improve organizational and individual performance. It will enable you to reach your quality goals

Exhibit 1-1. The quality roadmap.

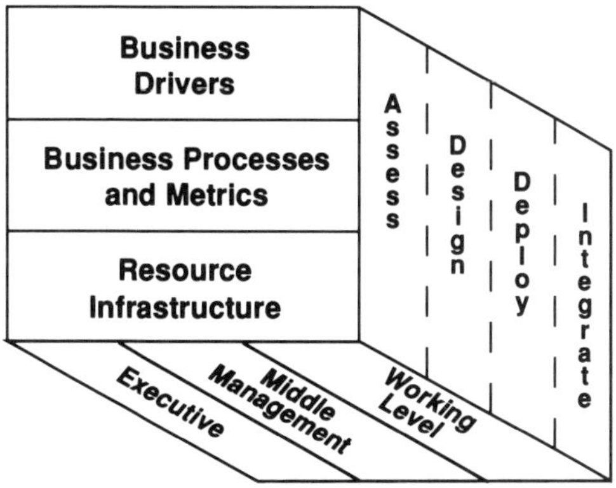

faster. Perhaps most important, the roadmap will allow you to step back and view your quality strategy within a larger, holistic systems context. Instead of exploring new territory blindly, chopping new roads with a machete, it permits a broader perspective. Using the roadmap as a diagnostic and planning tool, you'll be able to analyze how a given improvement will affect more than an isolated group, plant, or division; you will see how it might affect every one of your stakeholders and processes.

It will enable your quality effort to be driven by business strategy rather than TQM principles. You'll find yourself looking at quality logically, comprehensively, and sequentially. You'll view quality from the perspective of a business champion first, a quality champion second.

That higher, broader vision and the systematic progress toward achieving worthy business goals and strategies is what TQM is all about.

It's Also About People

With all this talk of processes and infrastructures, it's easy to forget the human factor. We believe that competent people are your most critical resource. No other resource can be maximized without competent people. PQM often neglects the real issues and needs of people—teams may be empowered to make improvements, yet if management does not deploy the right resources to make those improvements, or changes its strategy in midimprovement, people may become frustrated or demoralized or angry. The result: a lot of bitter people who grow to hate quality. We know of one company where the term *quality* has developed such a negative connotation that management now deliberately avoids its use in its TQM effort.

TQM and the roadmap mandate that people's needs be understood, respected, and met. As you'll see in the following chapters, the roadmap enables you to assess the impact of improvements on your people; it helps you allocate resources just in time, so that your employees are given the budget, staff, training, and other tools they need to get an improvement made; it not only motivates them to perform at their best, but creates an environment that optimizes their performance.

In Chapter 2, we'll provide you with more details on this map that will give your people an organized, connected, systematic environment in which to pursue quality goals for the sake of the business's performance.

Chapter 2

How the Roadmap Gets You to TQM Sooner and More Efficiently Than Any Other Tool

The evolution of our roadmap is instructive. Though we won't bore you with the mundane details of each step in its evolution, we think it's important that you understand the experiences and philosophies that shaped it. With that understanding, it will become clear why this map is a quality implementation tool for all organizations, regardless of the particular quality theory they espouse or the business goals to which they aspire.

We began working on the forerunner of this map in response to our clients' needs back in 1988. We watched as they were sidetracked and roadblocked by partial quality approaches. As they struggled through the improvement process, they asked if there was a better way.

We decided to find out. Our initial efforts focused on the Baldrige Award criteria. Though we found this to be a good measuring system, it didn't offer the structural framework necessary for implementing quality. As we examined and learned from other models and began working with other consultants, notably Jones, Reilly and Associates, the concept of the cube began to form. It gelled when we began our association with the Council for Continuous Improvement (CCI). Located in Silicon Valley, CCI was formed in 1989 by some of the country's top high-tech companies—National Semiconductor, Motorola, Texas Instruments, and many others. Their objective: to create a forum to allow member companies to learn from each other's experiences rather than reinventing the wheel in isolation. CCI recognized that some uniformity and order had to be imposed on the moving target of the quality movement. Without this, CCI's member companies were each exploring different paths in different ways—there was no common language, no meaningful way to exchange mutually beneficial information. In this environment, partial quality management was inevitable.

The roadmap cube was driven by not only CCI's needs but our own background and beliefs as management consultants. Human performance technology's basic tenet is that performance can be defined and measured, and that by systematically analyzing performance requirements we can redesign the organizational environment and select and train the people to achieve improved performance. If you provide people with the proper information, resources, skills, and consequences, they'll invariably be more productive. Years ago, performance technology was misinterpreted as being unproductively humanistic, placing the worker's job satisfaction above all else. It also ran counter to the prevailing sentiment at the time: that when companies have problems, people are to blame; that lazy, unmotivated people are the source of falling productivity and profitability.

Although organizations have become more enlightened about these matters over the years, some of the old prejudices still linger. But in our work with hundreds of clients, we've witnessed the efficacy of HPT. Case after case attests to the fact that the environment can be engineered and that people's behavior can be changed to produce better business results. Two statements capture this philosophy:

> "Take a good performer and put him in a bad system, and the bad system will win every time."—Geary Rummler, HPT pioneer
> "Eighty percent of all problems fall in the lap of management, because it's within management's control and authority." —W. Edwards Deming

It became our conviction that TQM is nothing more and nothing less than the management of all processes and systems to achieve business purpose and performance. And that the way to manage those systems is through a combination of HPT and the tools and techniques of the quality movement.

The roadmap cube reflects this combination. Before we explain each face of the cube, we should caution you that this isn't the final roadmap. It would violate our beliefs if it were not subject to its own continuous improvement (CI). But for now, it's the best planning and implementation tool for TQM of which we're aware.

The Front Face—The Business Architecture

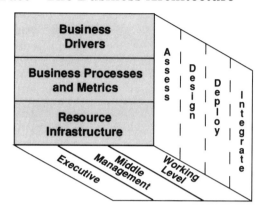

A recent experience with a client captures the significance of the cube's front face. We were sitting down with a CEO to discuss his TQM effort, and he had brought along a detailed outline of his proposed new organization structure, a structure that he wanted us to analyze. Before he showed us his organizational chart, we showed him a customized version of our roadmap cube. As soon as he looked at the front face, he put away the papers that contained his company's structure and said, "You've just given me a new way to think about organizing my company."

It's very difficult for organizations with a traditional pyramid structure to implement TQM. It's not only the top-heavy decision-making bureaucracy that creates problems, but the functional silos that divide the company. Cross-functional process optimization is crucial for the success of any TQM effort, but it's virtually impossible to produce cross-functional synergy when departments such as manufacturing and finance jealously guard their territory and exchange information with the wariness of cold war adversaries.

The front face effectively provides an alternative to the functional silo perspective. It helps companies organize their views and perspectives around processes—processes in which every department or division may participate regardless of its slot in the functional organizational hierarchy. Furthermore, your assets and competencies, marketplace and competitive factors, and balanced stakeholder requirements should drive the definition and metrics for the processes you have or should have in place. Process improvement requirements should flow from your stakeholder needs and strategic business goals, and not from some arbitrary or politically motivated goals list. Theoretically, this eliminates the archaic budget-allocation fights by functional vice-presidents, since business drivers (rather than clout or self-interest) determine where the resources go. Financial and other infrastructure resources, therefore, should be deployed and/or redeployed as driven by targeted and prioritized process improvements. Every resource, from people to information to dollars to equipment, is distributed according to what will best meet business performance improvement goals. Gone are the days when certain division heads and departments got what they wanted and others went begging.

Ultimately, what the front face of the cube does is redistribute power (via resources) more equitably and more effectively. In the new paradigm, people who receive power obtain what they need to accomplish the organization's improvement goals.

One last note about the front face: Notice that all processes are linked to an overall hierarchy of metrics tied to the business drivers. Establishing barometers for all processes is essential: Arbitrary, vague, or disconnected measurement systems aren't sufficient for identifying either improvement potential or improvement results. Every organization requires an overarching business measurement hierarchy, as shown in the middle section of the front face. Such metrics not only give you a realistic sense of how things are going, but allow you to put some meaning into the word *accountability*. Most organizations have only a partial measurement hierarchy, focusing heavily on short-term financial results.

The Four Phases

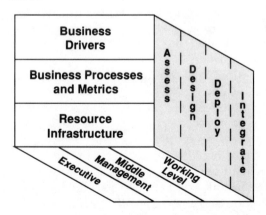

Assess. Design. Deploy. Integrate. These four phases will be familiar to anyone with a background in large-scale program or project management. But many people in top management come from sales, marketing, or finance and have little knowledge of complex, integrated project management. Everyone needs to acquire this knowledge—how to plan, organize, schedule, and track projects. Learning project management skills is necessary because quality implementation, like any major technical project, is highly complex. If you don't break the project down into its component parts and create a logical sequence for getting the job done, you'll be lost. Imagine if you attempted to build a new plant and decided to install the floor last instead of first. The same thing happens with TQM—people frequently do the right things at the wrong times.

The four phases facilitate the project planning and implementation process. They offer a tried-and-true sequence of activities. This sequence will teach you (among other things) that you should not deploy an improvement until you have pilot-tested it. Perhaps that seems obvious. But in the excitement and pressure of a TQM project, it's easy to spin out a potentially profit-enhancing improvement before it's been thoroughly tested.

The Three Organizational Levels

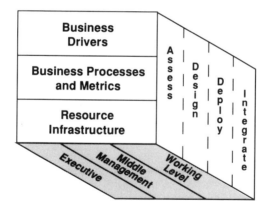

TQM isn't confined to a specific level of the organization, yet it's easy to neglect a level during a particular phase or in association with a certain process. The bottom face of the roadmap is designed to prevent this from happening.

Each level has a role to play. The executive level sets strategy, monitors progress, and does high-level project management taking a macro approach. The middle management or department level works cross-functionally in process areas such as product development or sales order entry and infrastructure areas such as information technology or training. The working level (teams and/or individual contributors) focuses on implementing the improvements, such as in a service center or production department, and making those many direct, small improvements that can only be made at ground level.

Putting It All Together

These three faces of the roadmap cube give organizations the ability to "mini-map" continuously. There are, in fact, 36 discrete mini-maps produced when you try every possible combination available: the three components of the front face, the four phases, and the three organizational levels. For instance, one mini-map would focus on Stakeholder Requirements/Assess/Working Level. Another would be Business Processes/Design/Middle Management. Within each of these mini-maps, you can create a series of even smaller maps—focusing on a particular business process, for instance.

To help you understand the benefits of this mapping, let us show you how one company employed our cube. The following is a condensation of steps taken during Phase 1, the assessment and planning phase at the executive level. The point of our taking you through this example is to give you a sense of how the map speeds your journey to TQM, minimizes false starts, and helps you properly allocate the resources required to make improvements possible. In other words, this is how a logical, comprehensive, and sequential approach can be used to implement TQM.

Company Q

Company Q is a medium-size manufacturer with six plants. For the past two years, it has implemented quality improvement programs in two of its plants' manufacturing areas. Though the improvements have been successful and saved the company money, the quality effort has been largely ad hoc and uncoordinated—partial rather than total quality management. When Company Q contacted us, it was stuck. It was unable to move improvements from one plant to another; it had made so many manufacturing improvements that it wasn't sure what making any more would gain it.

One of the first things we did was gather the information necessary to "map" or create the front face of the cube for Company Q. One of our primary information-gathering techniques consisted of one- to two-hour interviews with executives, middle managers, and employees involved with different processes. We asked approximately 75 people to:

- Define their particular process.
- Describe the critical inputs and outputs (enabling us to establish linkages between processes).
- List the stakeholders (and their needs) that relate to their process
- Suggest where there are disconnects with inputs and outputs.
- Provide their opinion about the potential for improvements in their process.

Based on the information we gathered, we created the map shown in Exhibit 2-1.

As you can see, this map presents only one segment of the cube's front face; the business drivers and resource infrastructure are absent. For now, though, let's examine only this segment to get a better understanding of the roadmap's dynamics.

First, this process breakout enables Company Q to start viewing its organization from a macro process perspective rather than a functional or departmental perspective.

Second, the act of mapping is revealing. In this case, Company Q discovered departments whose very existence was based on a negative premise: rework. As it tried to fit certain groups into a process and couldn't, it dawned on Company Q that these groups existed merely to correct mistakes. There were entire labs whose only purpose was to fix what other processes had broken.

Third, this map enables Company Q to see the linkages not only within product and service processes, but with the various leadership and support processes. In the past, Company Q had locked its improvement sights on manufacturing. It seemed logical to do so, since improvements in that area appeared to offer the biggest bang for the buck. Although this PQM approach did produce some cost and yield gains, those gains diminished over time. The problem, of course, was that improvements weren't being made to and/or deployed from other connected processes. If, for instance, sales volume increased, manufacturing would be in a better position to capitalize on its own improved speed and efficiency. Without the increase in sales volume, the improvement in manufacturing was limited.

Once the map has been done, an organization has a much easier

Exhibit 2-1. Company Q business processes.

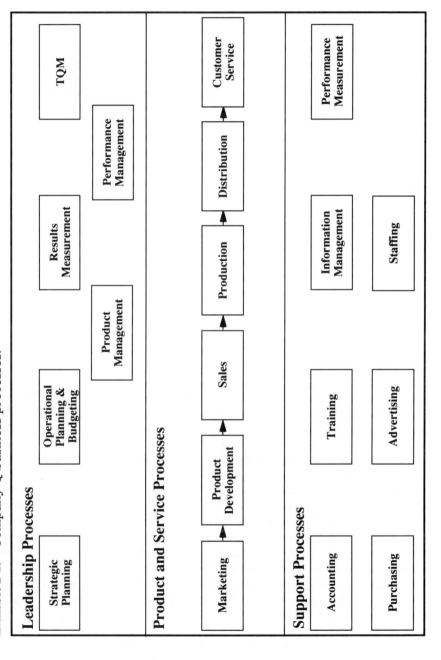

Leadership Processes

| Strategic Planning | Operational Planning & Budgeting | | Results Measurement | | TQM |
| | | Product Management | | Performance Management | |

Product and Service Processes

Marketing → Product Development → Sales → Production → Distribution → Customer Service

Support Processes

| Accounting | Training | | Information Management | Performance Measurement |
| Purchasing | Advertising | | Staffing | |

time identifying targets of opportunity. The knee-jerk reaction to target manufacturing or some other "easy" target doesn't happen. Instead, the map offers a broader, higher view that allows you to make educated decisions about improvement targets. This embodies management by facts or data rather than management by opinion.

Once company Q spotlighted these targets, we used the map to help it create a TQM team structure, which is shown in Exhibit 2-2.

The executive leadership team at the top of the chart and the leadership teams that cluster around the various processes are intended to be permanent. But as you can see on the chart, they spawn other "improvement teams," which work on specific projects—such as setting up a customer satisfaction measurement system, for instance—then go out of existence when those projects are completed.

Although Company Q had some experience with setting up teams, it found that our map helped set them up in a more effective, accountable manner. First, our structure ensured that there were no dangling teams. As you can see in Exhibit 2-2, every project improvement team is linked to at least one steering team. Every team is chartered, empowered, and held accountable by a linked team above it, and the limits of that empowerment are set. Every team has a sponsor, linking it to the team above that has leadership and support responsibility. Second, the support structure avoided the common problem of teams that are "all dressed up with nowhere to go." Without proper training, information, coordination with other teams, and additional resources, teams lose momentum. They may be empowered to make improvements, but they lack the support that realistically will make those improvements possible.

Next, we provided Company Q with a series of maps that take a closer look at each of its business processes. One example is the TQM process within Company Q's leadership processes (Exhibit 2-3).

In reality, process maps can be blown up to display increasing levels of detail until you get right down to the working-level tasks and steps. The trick is to connect these process maps in a hierarchy and to use the right level for the chosen improvement target. Within each process, certain issues must be addressed, certain actions taken. If, for instance, the leadership processes were to exclude the subprocess titled "Progress and Results Measurement," the people at the top would have little idea whether process improvements were actually taking place; they would be like generals without a command-and-control facility. These subprocesses provide every TQM team with a general sense of its responsibilities and tasks.

(Text continues on page 26)

Exhibit 2-2. TQM team structure.

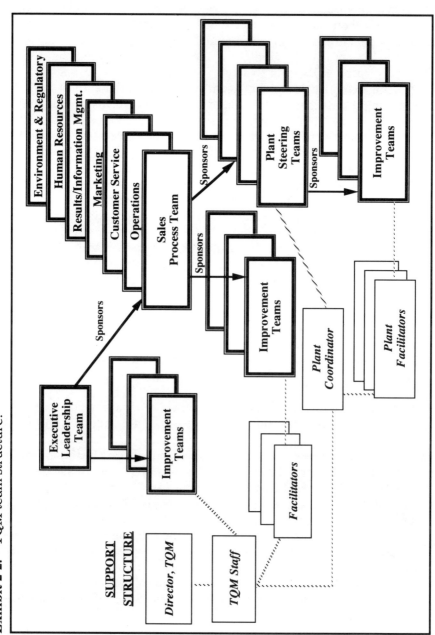

Exhibit 2-3. TQM processes.

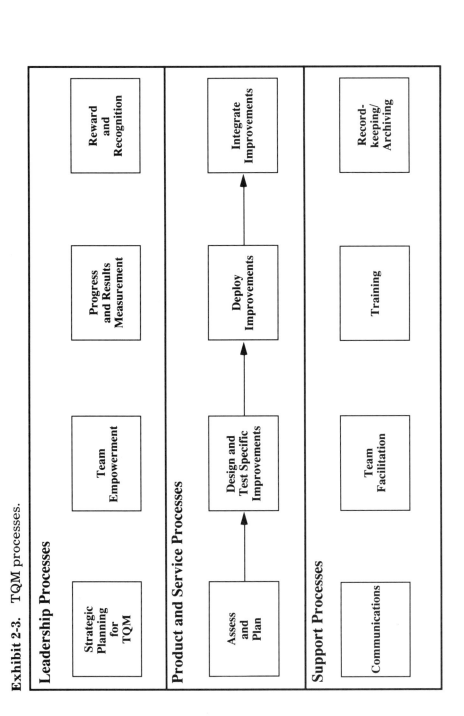

Although there are other aspects of the mapping process in Phase 1, such as input/output definition, the maps displayed here should give you a sense of how they facilitate TQM. For Company Q, they helped correct three common errors: (1) focusing on improvements that weren't strategic to the business, (2) failing to create improvement "energy" in any process outside of manufacturing, and (3) failing to notice the interdependence among major processes.

Better, Faster, Cheaper

One of the reasons the roadmap gets you to TQM without too many costly and time-consuming detours is that it starts you off properly in Phase 1. As the previous example demonstrated, the roadmap drives you to assess and plan your improvements comprehensively, so you don't leave key people or processes out of your strategy—missing people or processes can slow down or stop improvements. It also requires that an executive leadership team be formed, providing the necessary political buy-in and power to keep things moving and directed toward the real priorities of the business.

Finally, and perhaps most important, the challenge of TQM seems less overwhelming with the map in hand. What's often overwhelming is the thought of improving scores of processes simultaneously. The map dictates examining all these processes, but encourages selectivity in choosing the initial targets. You don't have to establish teams for nontargeted processes at first—just establish them for targets of opportunity. We believe that in a company's initial foray the "T" in TQM should be turned from Total to Targeted. With a targeted approach, good initial results build enthusiasm—enthusiasm that can sustain the effort down the road. Later, after all the truly significant quality improvements have been made (those with the greatest return dollars or strategic value), TQM can evolve to cover all processes and infrastructure elements.

As we've said before and we'll say again, TQM isn't simple. Similarly, this roadmap isn't a simple tool. If you're wondering how the roadmap will provide specific TQM direction for your organization, the next few chapters should provide some answers. Like any new tool, the roadmap requires patience and practice in order to master its use. That mastery begins with an understanding of your role in a TQM environment.

Chapter 3

A Map of the Territory— Locating Process Improvements and the Roads That Lead To and Fro

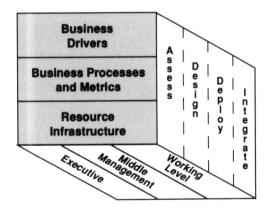

As you examine the front face of the roadmap, consider two fallacies that are common in organizations.

The first is that everyone has a good understanding of how the organization works. Typically, most individuals have a good understanding only of how their functional department works. When it comes to TQM, this narrow perspective can be a tremendous handicap. The CFO looks at improvements in terms of shareholder requirements; the sales manager considers them in light of customer requirements. Unfortunately, no one is seeing the bigger picture—the picture provided by the roadmap.

The front face of our roadmap cube forces everyone to think about improvements from a cross-functional, multidimensional perspective, a perspective that reflects how a business really works. All the issues that are so easily neglected in quality initiatives—multiple stakeholder requirements, human and environmental resources needed to facilitate specific process improvements, the linkages with leadership and support processes—can no longer be ignored.

The second fallacy is that the greater the number of improvements you make, regardless of their ROI, the better. This fallacy has been fostered by the Japanese, who continuously improve processes, even correcting relatively minor flaws in relatively minor processes. By and large, American companies don't have this luxury. We haven't been at this for twenty to forty plus years, as some Japanese companies have. We haven't improved all the major targets of opportunity. The Japanese are now forced to go after the smaller targets—over time they have become the largest remaining opportunities. We lack the resources to make improvements wherever and whenever possible. The fact that we try to do so accounts for empowered teams tackling "water cooler" improvements while more critical areas don't receive the attention they deserve.

Hygiene factors, such as location of water coolers, locker sizes, or restroom facilities, may in fact have a positive return on investment, but they typically are small potatoes compared with other opportunities. We believe that in the initial efforts to implement TQM, the acronym should stand for *targeted* quality management; it should later evolve into *total* quality management.

We need to see and prioritize improvement opportunities, and the front face of the map makes this possible. By the end of this chapter, you'll have an understanding of how you can use the map as a tool to assess your improvement opportunities within a business strategy context and plan effective improvement strategies. By the end of the book, you'll know how to combine this front face with the other roadmap faces to design, test, deploy, and integrate those improvements.

Let's begin with a basic premise that underlies this part of the map: You should manage your improvement strategy with facts and not opinions.

Objective vs. Subjective

Your business is inherently complex. Without a logical, comprehensive way to organize the data that pertain to your business, decisions will be made subjectively. Organizations frequently choose improvement targets for all the wrong reasons—politics, ease of making the improvement, influence of a quality guru, biases of top managers, and so on. In other words, improvement efforts are directed by someone's opinion, not by hard data.

The front face of our map gives you a way to organize your facts into discrete, usable parts. Once those facts are organized, you can then determine what process improvement can best help you achieve your business goals. For example, Company Q from Chapter 2 had been convinced that the way to reach its cost-reduction goal was through manufacturing gain-sharing programs and driving the cost out of the factory. This was a logical assumption, but an incorrect one. When Company Q examined the front face of its map, the missing link between manufacturing and sales appeared. When all the elements of these two processes were mapped, management saw that the factories were producing at a fraction of capacity, making the unit cost high because of the overhead that had to be overcome. The sales process, in turn, was in sad shape—it was breaking down because of outdated sales materials, too few high sales performers, and so on. But if the sales process were improved and sales volume increased, manufacturing volume would also increase and costs per unit would be driven down. The front face of the map helps you logically identify the "fulcrum points" for leveraging your investments in targeted quality improvements.

Establishing a Common Language

Couldn't Company Q have come to this conclusion without mapping its overall business? Maybe. But the map puts the improvement opportunity in a universally understandable language. Prior to mapping, Company Q's executive meetings were filled with agenda items such as new technology in plants, revamping training programs, and shareholder demands. Each item was the result of a functional opinion—the CFO was myopically focused on how to increase stock dividends in the next quarter, for instance. As a result, the agenda items were scattered and random; it was impossible to know which one deserved top priority.

Company Q was able to plug all its agenda items into the front face of its business map. Suddenly, there was a common language for talking about those items. Revamping training programs, for example, fit into the map's human resource infrastructure component and could be seen in the context of supporting and impacting the metrics of processes within the context of the business drivers. Taking away the functional bias and adding a comprehensive, connected view of its business allowed Company Q to determine that improving the sales process would give it the biggest bang for its buck in quality investment.

Establishing a common language also helps eliminate the confusion and misinterpretation that often accompany work on improvements, as the following story illustrates. We were at a meeting with a number of executives from a client company, and we were discussing the sales process. At one point in the discussion, some of the executives squared off, debating the merits of certain improvements versus others. The debate was going in circles, each side digging in. Eventually, we figured out the source of the problem: One group of executives was defining the sales process differently from the other group. The first group defined the process as everything from the front-end effort needed to make the sale to the back-end follow-up after the sale. The second group was limiting its definition to all activities until the sale was made.

Quality efforts run into brick walls because processes are complex and boundaries between processes are typically undefined, giving rise to varying interpretations of processes. We've seen top managers in an organization who have very different ideas about whether a process falls into the support or the product/services category. In some companies, managers aren't even aware of what the leadership processes are or have never categorized their activities that way. Similarly, there may be ten different views of what groups are stakeholders. Infrastructure often goes undefined or is not linked to process performance. Our observation is that even companies that are engaged in major improvement initiatives and that understand the importance of focusing on customer requirements and on cross-functional process improvement do not have a complete macro picture of the business to use as a basis for assessment and improvement planning.

TQM can't tolerate imprecise or ill-defined organizations. Without a universal language and understanding of how the company works, confusion and PQM are inevitable. As in the previous example, when one person talks about the sales process, another person conjures up a set of activities different from those the speaker intended to communicate. Imagine these frequently silent misunderstandings multiplied many times over and you'll glimpse the seriousness of the problem.

Miscommunication often translates into overlaps or gaps between processes during the implementation phase. We've found that it's common for two teams within an organization to be duplicating efforts—they're both working on the same improvement in the same way, but since no one clarified what Team A and Team B should do, overlap results. Similarly, teams can be ignoring a critical aspect of an improvement because no one has defined process boundaries with any clarity—Team A thinks Team B should be working on the improvement, and Team B thinks Team A should be working on it.

If your business has been mapped out in detail as this chapter suggests, these gaps and overlaps will be rare.

Demystifying the Three Elements

The map's front face can be confusing or even intimidating to those who are used to looking at their business from traditional perspectives. No question, there's a lot here, especially for organizations that are used to more familiar functional organization charts. But we think you'll find this approach both comprehensible and usable when you've completed this chapter.

What this front face recommends is also quite different from what many other quality approaches ask you to do. Typically, quality initiatives focus on customer requirements and process improvement exclusively, setting numerous teams off on numerous process improvement assignments. The business drivers segment is largely ignored except for customers; the infrastructure resources are also often overlooked, except for the most obvious things such as money and equipment. Or if they're not overlooked and ignored, they're treated haphazardly. There is often no strategic approach to integrating all these factors, no connections established between the many elements on the front face. Without an integrating mechanism, PQM is inevitable.

This front face allows you to put your business "theory" into focus—what drives your organization and how it does so. Some companies that used to be models of success have been having many problems because they can't quite get that theory articulated, disseminated, and commonly understood. Here, you can map it out for everyone to see. When you map your process using this front face, you can evaluate it from all angles: Is the problem with a process the lack of a key competency? Is it failing to satisfy critical stakeholder requirements? Is a new competitor changing the rules of the process game so that you have to make a major improvement or lose share? Are the human and environmental resources necessary for a planned improvement in place? You can determine and communicate the full set of implications before attempting to improve any process.

Before we start our demystification process, let us answer one question that occurs to many people when they start working with the roadmap: Where should we start? The best approach we know of is to do a rough map of the entire front face, which should not take very long. Then use this map to make an overall assessment of business performance and determine which areas of the map represent the most promising targets of opportunity. Start the improvement process by focusing mainly on these targeted areas. Our chapter on Phase 1 covers this approach in much more detail.

Eventually, you will have continuous improvement efforts going on in all areas of the front face map.

Business Drivers

Business drivers are divided into three categories or issue sets that determine business success: assets and competencies, stakeholders' requirements, and marketplace and competition. An easy way to think of these is shown in Exhibit 3-1. They represent your ability to play in the game of business, the object(s) of the game, and the playing field and rules of the game. Obviously, these are highly interactive. Arranging these elements for success is typically the object of the strategic planning and marketing processes.

The assets and competencies and the marketplace and competitive factors are much easier to explain than the stakeholders' requirements, so let's deal with these two categories first.

Assets and competencies represent the capability of the organization to perform in the marketplace. They are business drivers because in pursuing any business goal, they represent both opportunities or strengths and limitations or weaknesses.

Assets and competencies can include any of the following:

- Patents and other intellectual property
- Methods (e.g., information management)
- Technologies (e.g., genetic engineering, imaging, etc.)
- Natural resources (e.g., land, oil, water rights)
- Physical capability (e.g., a worldwide airline fleet)
- Financial capability (e.g., $6 billion in cash reserves)
- Human capability (e.g., a world-class R&D lab in telecommunications)
- Information (e.g., a comprehensive customer preference database)

You can identify your assets and competencies by asking questions such as: What are we good at? What's our capacity? What factors give us a competitive edge?

Exhibit 3-1. Categories of business drivers.

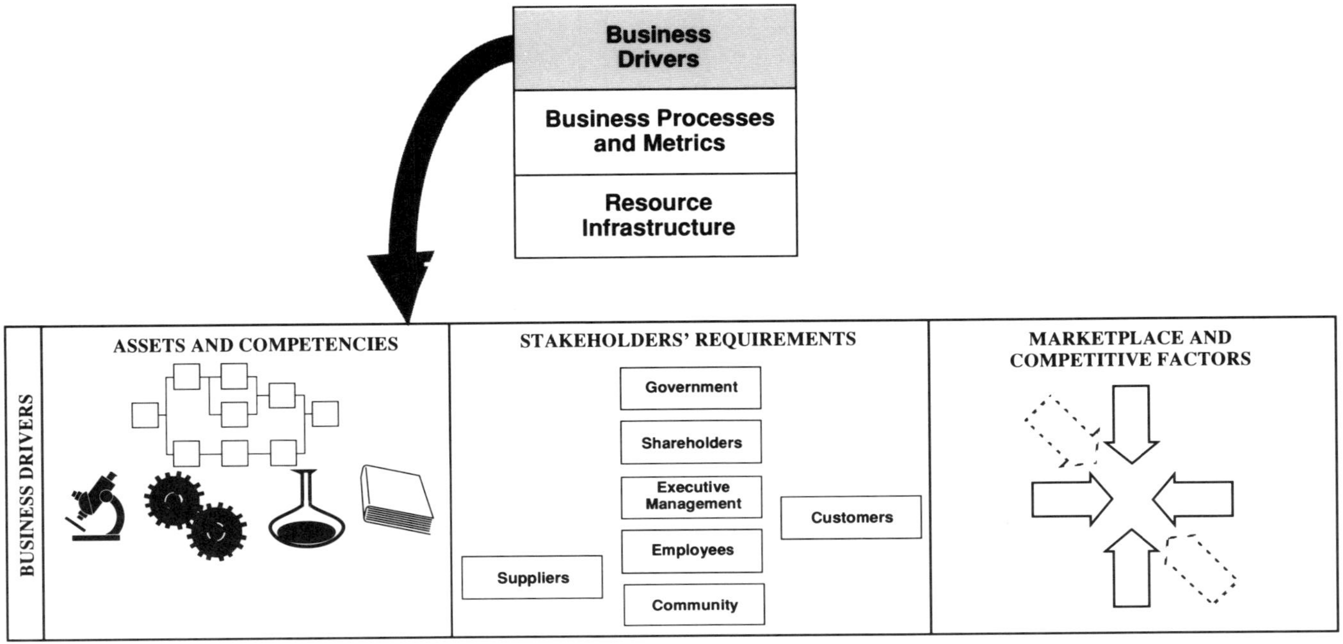

BUSINESS DRIVERS

Business Drivers

Business Processes and Metrics

Resource Infrastructure

ASSETS AND COMPETENCIES

STAKEHOLDERS' REQUIREMENTS

Suppliers

Government

Shareholders

Executive Management

Employees

Community

Customers

MARKETPLACE AND COMPETITIVE FACTORS

Organizations sometimes overlook certain assets and competencies. If you have a great deal of cash, those deep pockets may be a very important asset. Your location at a transportation hub that reduces delivery costs may be another. Include here everything that you can think of, whether or not it's being actively capitalized upon. When you reach the map's process section, you may find that a previously overlooked asset comes in handy.

Marketplace and competitive factors define the playing field. Marketplace and competitive factors should include:

- Competition
- Scientific knowledge
- Social and cultural climate (e.g., growing intolerance for pollution, increasing openness to business in the former Soviet Union)
- Economic factors (e.g., world, country, and local economy)
- World-class benchmarks (e.g., best-in-class performance on package delivery speed and accuracy)
- Infrastructural factors (e.g., transportation, telecommunications)
- Laws and regulations
- Technology status and rate of change

Defining these drivers is more than a mere exercise. If your organization is like most of those we've worked with, your people have different perspectives on what constitute competitive factors and assets. In one organization, some members of the executive leadership team viewed the company's state-of-the-art technology as an asset, since it helped the company achieve a leadership position in a product category; others, however, viewed it as a liability because the technology had made the company complacent and it had done little research in new technologies that had much more earnings potential than the current technology. Similarly, we've seen companies where there was little agreement about the competition—some executives viewed Company A as the only real competition, whereas others perceived Companies B, C, and D to be just as dangerous. Major confusion over business drivers may be a signal that the strategic planning and marketing processes are not working well.

By clarifying these issues via the map, you avoid miscommunication that can misdirect process improvements down the road. Focus improvements on areas that will give you a real competitive advantage. Improving production capacity in an oversupplied market is inappropriate.

Now let's turn to the more complex stakeholder requirements—

we've listed requirements of seven of the most common stakeholder categories. Remember, meeting these requirements is the object of the game. As you can see, government is placed at the top and the community is placed at the bottom of our chart. That doesn't mean that the community's requirements are insignificant; it simply means that the government's demands are generally more complex and in many cases impossible to ignore. When you're trying to resolve conflicts between stakeholders (as we'll discuss in a bit), it would be wise to consider where each of your stakeholders sits on your particular stakeholder hierarchy.

Next, map your stakeholders' specific requirements using the following starter list of requirement categories. If there are requirement categories missing that are particularly relevant to your organization, by all means add them and then detail the specifics of the requirements.

Government

- Health/safety
- Environment
- Tax law
- Employment and labor relations
- Securities law and regulations
- Industry-specific regulations

Shareholders

- Long-term returns (growth in the value of shareholders' equity)
- Short-term returns (net income)
- Alignment with societal norms (equal opportunity, environmental issues)

Executive management

- Progress toward long-term business goals and strategies
- Progress toward short-term business goals and strategies
- Company reputation with shareholders, customers, and the investment community

Customers

- Product features, quality, and price
- Service features, quality, and price
- Pricing/payment terms
- Future needs
- Response time

Employees

- Job security
- Competitive wages and benefits
- Safety
- Opportunities for personal challenge and growth

Suppliers

- Continuity of business
- Level-loaded demand for their products or services and advance warning of peaks and valleys
- Profitability

Community

- Environmental impact
- Economic impact
- Safety
- Infrastructure impact
- Social contribution

Balancing all these requirements isn't easy, especially when conflicts exist. And when you begin planning improvements, you'll see the potential conflicts—not only between different categories of stakeholders, but within the same category (between two groups of employees, for instance). Conflicts between requirements that may have simmered on the back burner under the old system are brought into the open by TQM; you will have to decide whose requirements are met and whose are not, and this invariably causes problems—unless you communicate the "whys" of the tradeoff in terms that those affected can understand.

In Chapter 6, we'll look at the linking of stakeholder requirements to assets and competencies and the marketplace and competitive factors. For now, though, you should simply look over your requirements list with your planned process improvements in mind. Focus on one such improvement and ask yourself the following questions:

- What stakeholder values are affected positively and negatively?
- Which stakeholders are crucial to the improvement process's success? What is the rank order of importance of each stakeholder group?
- What can you do to gain their support for the improvement? What involvement strategies can you create for different groups to ensure their enthusiastic participation?

- How can you resolve potential conflicts between groups through negotiation, persuasion, and the clarification of each group's requirements and the impacts of meeting or not meeting them?

Answering these questions enables you to assess your leadership processes with much greater awareness of cutting-edge issues. When you're called upon to create a strategic plan or allocate resources, you can do so with stakeholder requirements and potential conflicts in mind.

Before we conclude this section, let us issue a few words of warning about one particular stakeholder: The customer is not king. At least, the customer is not king if this means treating the other stakeholders like insignificant peasants. Yet in many companies aspiring to implement a quality improvement effort, we see management disseminating slogans that suggest that customer requirements are the top and absolute priority. The quality movement has rightfully reminded us not to be so arrogant as to ignore our customers' needs and desires. An unfortunate repercussion of this single-minded customer emphasis, however, has been the failure to understand the legitimate and important requirements of our other stakeholders. If in your quest to fulfill customer needs for faster, cheaper, and better service you violate government regulations, disrupt the external community, and antagonize the union, your improvement efforts will most likely fail. As you examine all your stakeholder requirements in light of improvement opportunities, keep these two points in mind:

1. *Focusing exclusively on meeting all customer needs can waste shareholders' equity.* Satisfying all customer requirements can be very costly. Although in the short term customers may be pleased to have optimized their situation, such a focus may hurt the suppliers' profitability and could eventually have a negative impact on those customers. Continually meeting customer requirements better than the competition does—and meeting them in a way that achieves business metrics—is a more appropriate goal.

2. *Catering exclusively to customers can turn employees against TQM.* To meet customer demands, companies may have to work employees longer and harder; downsizing may be necessary; disruptive transfers may be common. This all means change, and change, while necessary, may be painful. If employees perceive TQM to mean that customers get everything and they get nothing, they will sabotage the effort, and no amount of talk about partnerships, cooperation, or mutual benefit will help. The concept of partnership is working together for real mutual benefit.

If all players involved in a quality effort don't share a common vision of the business drivers, confusion and conflict result.

Ultimately, management will have no choice but to suspend work on quality improvement efforts, and the quality initiative will be widely viewed within the company as a failure. Employees will resent it, shareholders will be aghast at the costs without the returns, and other stakeholders will probably be similarly upset. It's at this point that people begin saying, "TQM doesn't work." But it's not TQM that doesn't work, it's partial quality management that doesn't work.

Although we've focused primarily on stakeholder requirements here, don't ignore the other two groups of drivers. All three must be considered for TQM efforts to be targeted and implemented effectively.

Business Processes and Metrics

Most organizations are capable of mapping their mainstream product and service processes and establishing metrics, so we're not going to bore you with what you already know. If you do need help, a good source is *Improving Performance* by Geary Rummler and Alan P. Brache. We assume that you're reasonably adept at mapping a process from inputs to outputs, measuring that process, and conducting gap analysis (between where a process is now and where it could be). Most of you can also intuitively spot major processes in need of improvement, especially on your first pass through the map—the big improvement targets are hard to miss (though targets become increasingly more difficult to find on each pass through the map).

These understandings alone will only get you to PQM. TQM requires other, often neglected exercises, which this part of the map suggests, including:

- Establishing your business measurement hierarchy
- Placing business processes in three categories and establishing connections with targeted process improvement
- Examining business/service process improvements relative to business drivers and resource infrastructure

It's astonishing how often the total business measurement hierarchy is neglected or misused in improvement planning and implementation. In Exhibit 3-2 we've listed three of the most common business measurements: financial, customer satisfaction, and employee satisfaction. If an organization formally measures only financial performance, for instance, then improvements will probably be myopically targeted

Exhibit 3-2. Categories of business processes and metrics.

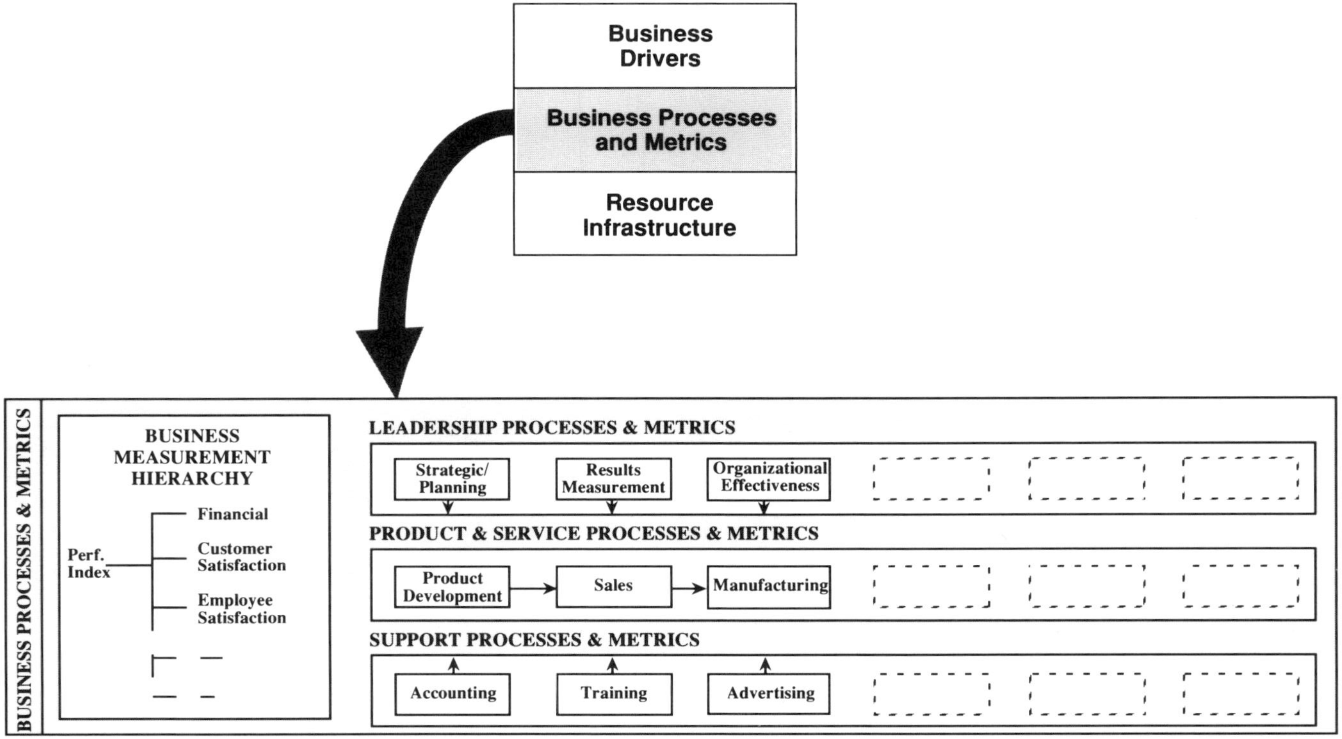

and monitored to satisfy only shareholders and no other stakeholder group. In this case, if customer satisfaction is not considered, ultimately the monitored results will meet no one's requirements. Or it may be that nothing except the highest-level financial performance is formally measured—a hazy, ill-defined measurement system means that no one is sure what type of performance is monitored or rewarded, allowing improvements to go forward without any clear direction.

Determining what your organization measures and how those measurements are linked together is absolutely necessary. When you're aware of how a process improvement meets financial, customer satisfaction, and employee satisfaction measures, you're in a much better position to assess and plan for that improvement.

Next, the map calls for you to divide your processes into three categories. We have also listed some of the typical processes found in each of the three.

- *Leadership processes*: strategic planning, operational planning, budget control, empowerment, and results measurement
- *Products and services processes*: research, development, marketing, sales, order fulfillment, production, process and facility maintenance, customer service
- *Support processes*: human resources, finance, information management

This categorization accomplishes a number of objectives. First, it prevents anyone from treating a support process like a product or service process. We've seen quality initiatives encounter difficulties because support processes were optimized at the expense of suboptimizing a product or service process. The simple rule here is: Treat support processes as they were intended, to support mainstream processes. They don't exist for their own purposes. A common view of this relationship is required by all parties for continuous process improvement decision making.

These categories also provide you with an organizing tool, critical in the complex world of TQM. They make connections within and between the three groupings visible. If you've determined that it's essential for the business to make an improvement in production, you can see how that improvement will be facilitated or inhibited by the other product and service processes and support processes, you can analyze what should be done in a leadership process such as strategic planning to get that improvement on track, and you can make adjustments in a support process like human resources to recruit people with certain skills for a production improvement team.

Creating these back-and-forth process linkages enables TQM to proceed in an organized, coherent fashion. TQM efforts can be "engineered" in this manner. You lessen the likelihood of dangling teams where there is great confusion and inability to make coherent business decisions with confidence—the curse of many quality programs. As you create your macro maps of this front face, always remember that every item on your maps must be connected to something else. Every process, no matter what category it's in, must be clarified in terms of the inputs and outputs that link it with other processes.

The linkages, of course, don't stop here. Process improvements have to be considered within the context of the business drivers and resource infrastructure boxes. Let's say your executive leadership team has targeted the distribution process for improvement. You have to map out this targeted process not only from beginning to end, not only from leadership to support processes, but from where the process inputs originate to where the process outputs lead. How will a proposed improvement affect all the stakeholder groups (not just customers)? Will suppliers be capable of providing materials to meet the new deadlines? How will shareholders accept the huge forecasted capital equipment expenditure? In terms of inputs, how may each leadership and support process facilitate or inhibit achieving the distribution process improvement goal? What data will distribution people require to meet the new delivery time frames? Is the company's MIS system capable of providing them with these data when they need them and in the correct form? In terms of outputs, how will faster delivery times affect the manufacturing process? Will they impose impossible deadlines on a manufacturing system that hasn't been improved in years?

There are hundreds of connections that must be understood and refined for every improvement. Some are obvious; most are subtle. Mapping them exposes connections that would otherwise escape notice.

Now let's look at how the front face of the cube establishes the connections between an improvement and the infrastructure.

Resource Infrastructure

Our fishbone diagram of the infrastructure (Exhibit 3-3) contains ten "bones" (rather than the Ishakawa diagram's four): four on the human resource side and six on the environmental resource side. Each of these infrastructure issues must be examined relative to a proposed improvement.

Exhibit 3-3. Fishbone diagram of the resource infrastructure.

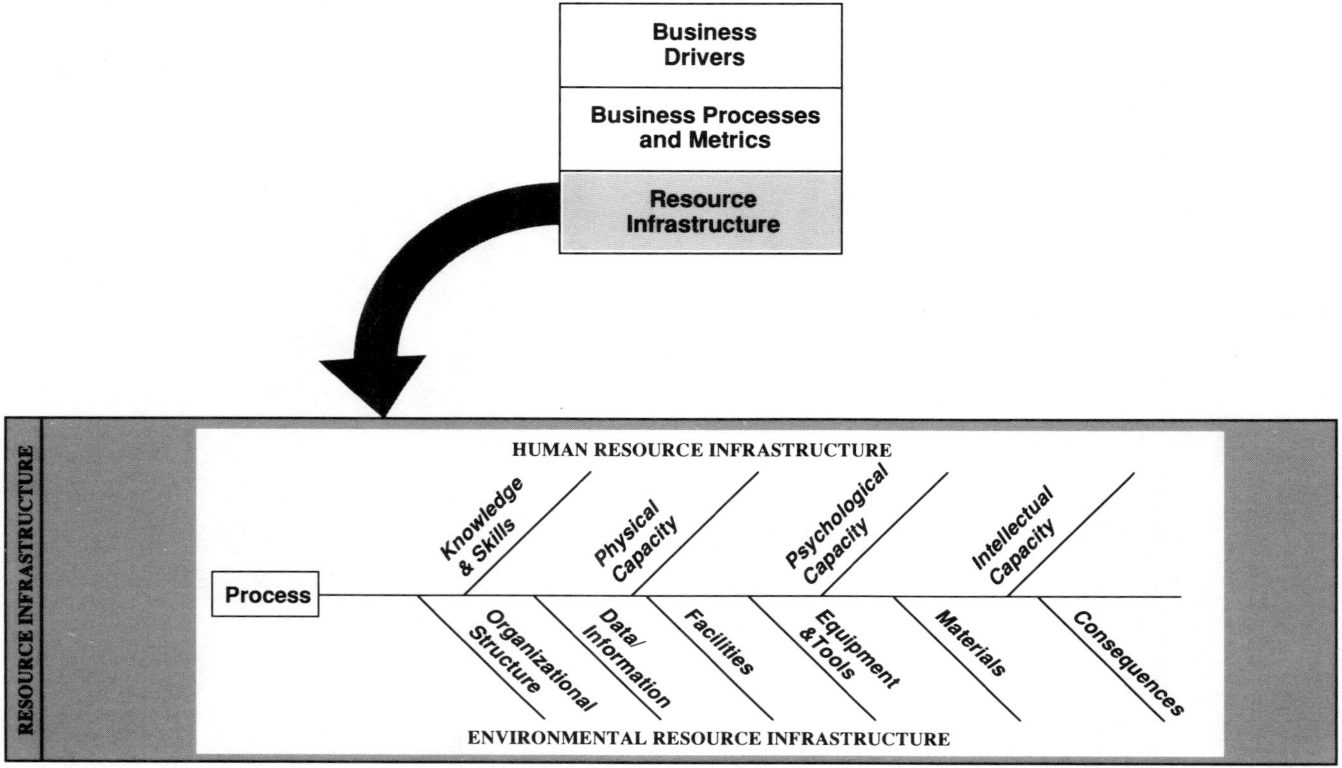

Without this map, it's difficult to ascertain all the investment and return figures and to allocate your resources so that they support a targeted improvement that promises a sufficient return. Typically, your plan will come up short in some of the resource categories. Without this fishbone diagram in hand, your focus is on the targeted process—when you're in the boiler room tinkering with a balky engine, you don't see that the ship is heading for an iceberg. Focusing exclusively on the process, you won't discover what else might require change until it's too late—or at least until you've squandered precious time and money only to find that you lack the overall resources necessary to really make an improvement happen. And perhaps with a more complete view of the investment costs and the returns, you will reaim your efforts elsewhere.

We have identified ten key resource infrastructure categories, each of which can have a significant impact on your improvement's success or failure. While some infrastructure resources are obvious—a new, improved plant mandates a larger physical space and more sophisticated equipment—many are subtle. Our fishbone, or your customized version of it, will act as a common thinking guide for uncovering the realities of both the status quo and the desired state.

Without careful selection and training, your employees may not be equipped to handle the stress that an improved process brings. It's easy to overlook an employee skill set that's essential for facilitating an improvement. You may have a balance of consequences that drives a certain type of behavior (for example, individual goal achievement is rewarded more often than team goal achievement), and this balance may be counterproductive to process improvements.

Scores of infrastructure changes may be necessary, and the map helps you understand, organize, and prioritize them.

The map also helps you make the right infrastructure changes rather than the wrong ones. We know of an organization that decided it had to improve product quality through a manufacturing process re-vamp. It spent millions of dollars purchasing state-of-the-art equipment for this improvement, but product quality improved only marginally. The problem: The employees lacked the training, knowledge, skills, and attitudes necessary to work productively in the new factory environment. The company later established a hiring/training and certification program that brought in new people with the necessary skills and retrained the existing staff. The upgraded plant then achieved the results it was capable of. Failure to plan for work force skill development as part of a change initiative is an extremely common error.

Again, connections cut across the entire front face of the cube. If an improvement calls for increased capital expenditures, you must examine those expenditures relative to different stakeholder requirements: How will industry analysts react and how will the news be presented to them? Will the expenditure require a freeze on hiring? The infrastructure decision should also be viewed from the perspective of all the drivers. If a new information system is called for, then it may be wise to check out world-class examples of this type of system.

When you're mapping the infrastructure requirements for a process improvement, remember to assess all ten bones in the diagram. That doesn't mean you have to marshall new resources for each of them. But by assessing all ten areas, you can prioritize each resource according to which ones will contribute most to improvement goals.

Starting Out on the Right Foot

Many quality initiatives end up going nowhere or going off course because of errors made in the planning stage. This front face helps you see your improvement targets clearly and in totality. When you create all the macro maps dictated by this face and establish the many connections that may otherwise have been hidden from view, you can see the roadblocks before you hit them. It suddenly becomes clear that if the training component of your support process isn't addressed, you'll never be able to make your desired customer service process improvement. The map may reveal that if you embark on certain manufacturing improvements to please customers, you may risk a union strike because the represented employees won't like the new working hours dictated by the improvements. Not that this would stop you cold; but rather understanding this should change your assessments, strategies, and tactics.

When we've introduced this front face of the map to clients, their reaction has been: "Before, we looked at our business from ground level and our vision was limited; your map gives us a higher, broader perspective." The more you see, the faster and easier it is to navigate through the complicated maze of highways leading to TQM.

It's also faster and easier when each organizational level is accounted for in the TQM journey. Chapter 4 will explain the bottom face of the roadmap cube, and how it fits with the front face.

Chapter 4

Organizational Levels

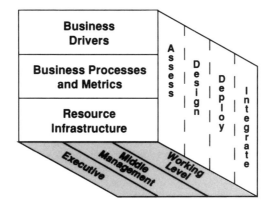

We typically look at three different levels of improvement activity on the bottom face of our cube: the executive, middle management, and working levels. Three is by no means the definitive number; some organizations will remap this face to have two, some will have five. However many levels your organization has, you'll find that these categories cover most of the territory—even organizations with ten or more levels can fit them into these three general categories.

If this aspect of the roadmap seems obvious in theory, let us assure you that it is not obvious in practice. Because TQM is complex, key people can easily be left out of an improvement or can perform inappropriate and duplicated tasks. By juxtaposing these three levels against the front face of the cube, you don't easily leave anyone or anything out of the improvement process. You guard against partial quality management with this holistic approach.

Different types of improvement activities are appropriate at each level. At the executive level, the activity is strategic. At the middle management level, it's translating strategies into operational changes and tactics. At the working level, it's implementing tactics. Examine the front face of the cube in terms of the designated type of activity. If you're at the executive level, for instance, you have a far different perspective on the drivers, processes, and infrastructure than someone at the working level. That is appropriate.

What is the benefit of these different perspectives? Or, more to the point, what is the cost if we do not continuously use these different levels and carefully integrate across them to define our TQM activities?

Without an understanding of the effects of our targeted improvement effort on the different levels, or an understanding of the roles and responsibilities we need to deploy at these levels, you'll never be able to translate your executive improvement strategy into actual improvements. If your working level does manage to make an improvement, it may have very little to do with your strategy.

If, however, you pay attention to the levels and the linkages between levels, you can deploy both your strategic intent and the requisite resources to ensure that improvements are strategic and beneficial.

The Missing Middle Level

Here is a typical scenario that illustrates how strategy is separated from improvements. Top management gets the quality religion and begins its TQM effort with great gusto. Executives establish the mission and values of the effort; they establish teams at the working level and launch a massive training program. Although these teams may be numerous, trained, and empowered, they begin work on improvements in an almost ad hoc fashion—no one is guiding or supporting their efforts. Because they're left to their own devices when it comes to choosing improvement targets, they often choose ones of self-interest: the "water cooler" projects that will make their lives easier or that optimize only their part of the world, rather than the projects that management has determined are strategically best for the company or that optimize the whole, sometimes at the seeming expense of a portion.

It's remarkably easy to leave middle management out of an improvement program. In some cases, the decision to destratify the organization is responsible. In other cases, it's because all the "action" seems to take place at the working team level, giving middle management little to do.

The bottom face of the cube forbids you to ignore the middle level. It is in the best position to take executive strategy, translate it into usable terms for the working-level teams, and plan how those teams can best approach an improvement opportunity. The tough jobs of allocation of limited resources and monitoring resource reallocation requirements, as well as adjudicating tradeoffs in decision making, are key.

The middle level should not only help information flow down, but should also help it flow back up and/or over. For instance, an improvement is successfully piloted at the working level in a plant. The manufacturing middle-level team sees the excellent results and can deploy this improvement in six other plants. The middle level is crucial for the deployment phase of the roadmap, and if this level of activity is neglected, a successful pilot improvement may not successfully be deployed to other areas of opportunity. The result: PQM.

A neglected middle level means that you will typically have no real way to measure whether an improvement worked or didn't or whether resources were properly expended. Besides translating strategy and planning improvements, middle managers can function as improvement barometers. The executive level is too removed and the working level is too close to the action to measure progress accurately. Metrics are crucial to TQM, and the middle level is best suited to keep track of those metrics.

The middle management level is where the focus on major process improvements occurs. For example, middle-level team structures may be formed to deal with improvements in process sets such as product development, distribution, and sales and marketing. The executive level can't put in the time, attention, and effort required, and the working level doesn't have a high enough vantage point.

In many ways, the middle level of activity is the most challenging, since anyone working at that level is called upon to abandon a "silo" mentality and work cross-functionally. Anyone who is involved in middle-level activity has to guard against reverting to a functional mentality—you can't translate management direction to working teams unless you think in terms of cross-functional processes and doing what is best for the company as a whole rather than what is best for a department.

A Matter of Detail

We'd like to show you perspectives on the sales process from three different levels.

As you can see from Exhibit 4-1, the executive point of view identifies the sales process as one process amid our three groups of

Exhibit 4-1. Business processes: the executive-level point of view.

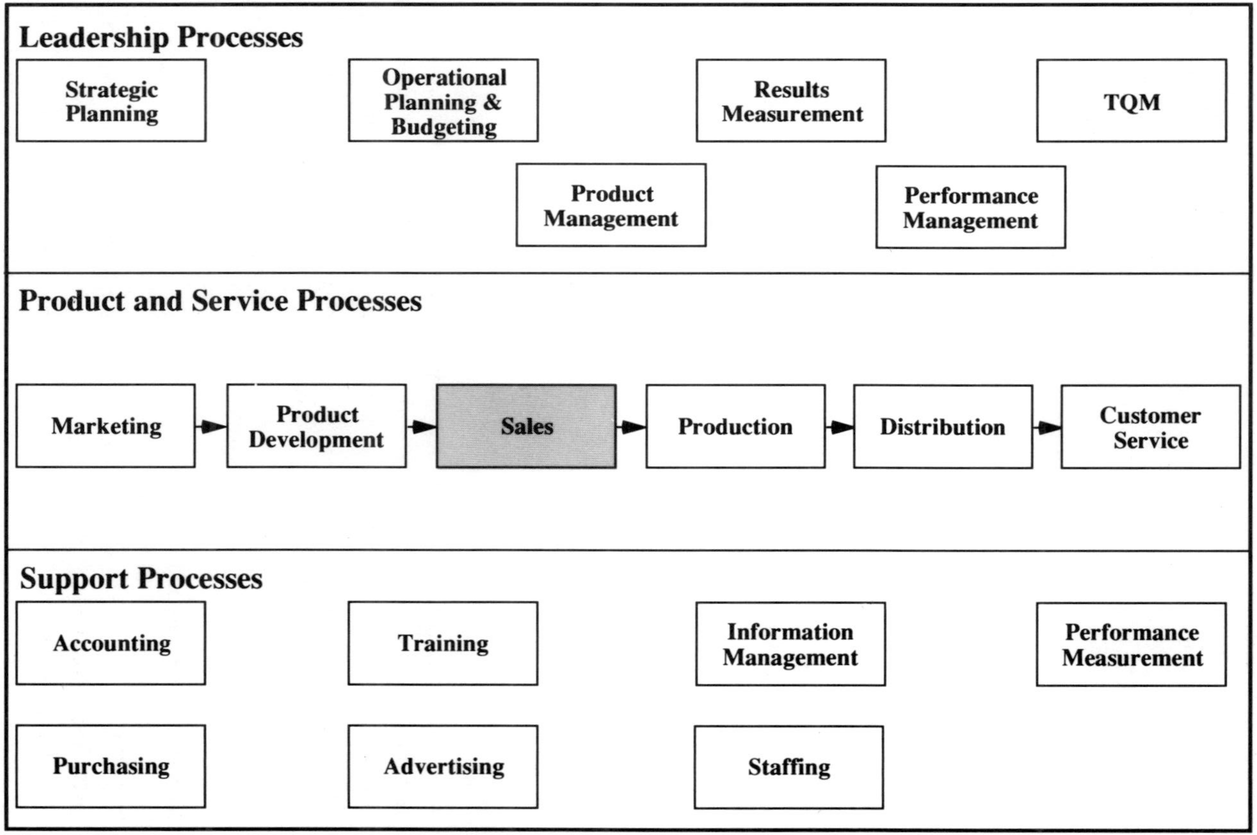

Leadership Processes

| Strategic Planning | Operational Planning & Budgeting | Results Measurement | | TQM |

| | | Product Management | Performance Management | |

Product and Service Processes

Marketing → Product Development → Sales → Production → Distribution → Customer Service

Support Processes

| Accounting | Training | Information Management | Performance Measurement |

| Purchasing | Advertising | Staffing | |

processes. From the middle management perspective (Exhibit 4-2), this process is broken down into a number of discrete subprocesses, each representing a major part of the sales process. At the working level, one of the subprocesses from the middle management chart, order entry, is deconstructed in Exhibit 4-3 as multiple, connected steps.

As the charts make clear, the amount of detail increases dramatically as you move down through the levels. Delineating the amount of detail helps focus each level appropriately—executives don't get unnecessarily bogged down in detail, and implementation teams appropriately create maps that put all the real-world details into an orderly, connected flow.

By looking at all improvement opportunities from multiple levels, you accomplish the following:

- Avoiding duplication of effort or gaps (where a critical assignment is overlooked)
- Providing a holistic way of looking at total quality
- Linking the inputs and outputs of people and processes at one level to the inputs and outputs of people and processes at another level

Consider multiple-level perspectives within the context of the roadmap's front face. Your type of activity will determine what you take away from this particular view of this face. In terms of stakeholder requirements, for instance, the executive level may be very concerned about satisfying shareholder needs for long-term growth via an improvement, while a working-level team will be focused on tailoring its improvement tasks to detailed customer specs. The executive view of the map is strategic; the working-level view is tactical. Unless all the levels are integrated, there's nothing to prevent a working-level team from imposing its own strategic spin, or to prevent top mangement from intruding at the tactical level.

In short, levels keep everyone focused on improvement activities appropriate to their levels and roles within the organization.

Level Relationships

In TQM, employees and teams must consider their actions in relation to the actions of other employees and teams. We've seen too many quality programs weakened by "lone rangers"—executives who tried to make

(Text continues on page 52)

Exhibit 4-2. Sales processes: the middle-management-level point of view.

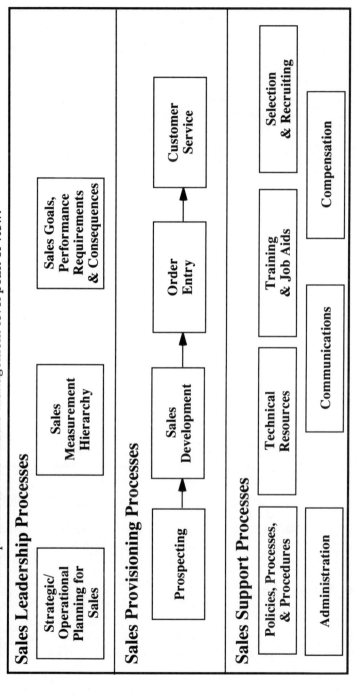

Exhibit 4-3. Sales order entry: the working-level point of view.

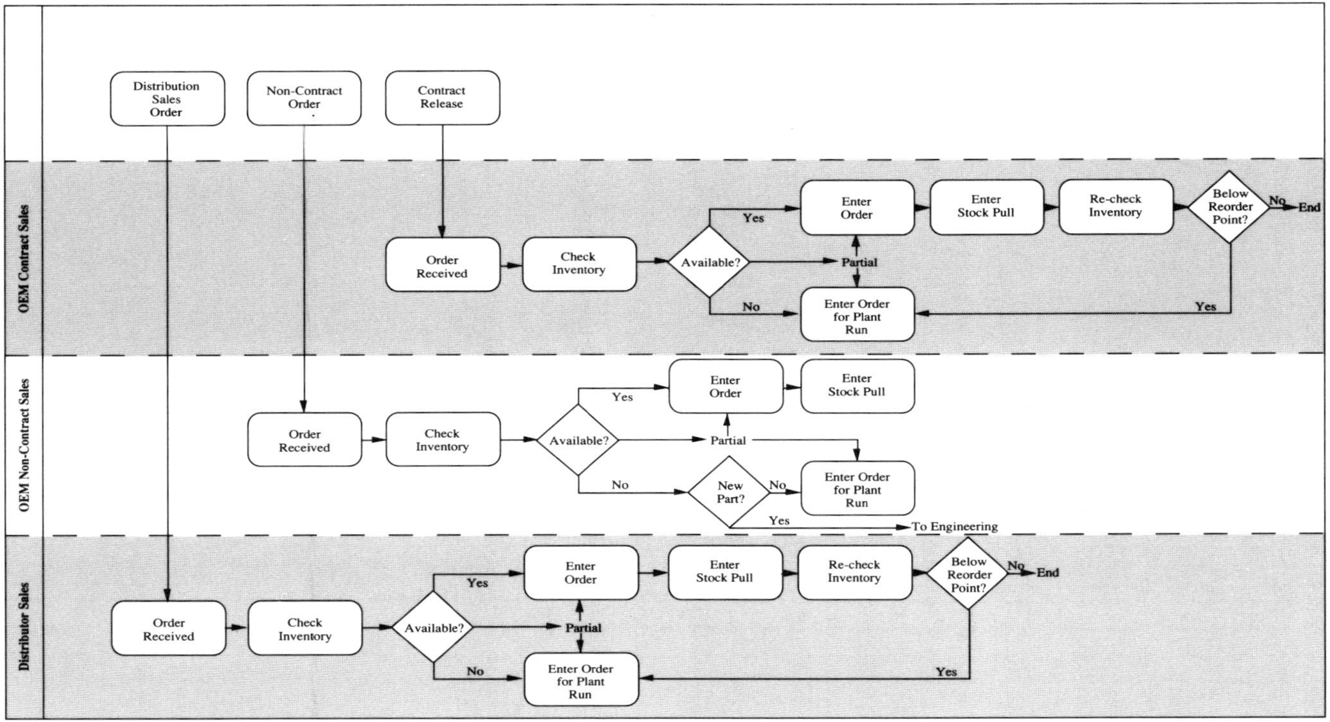

improvements single-handedly rather than holistically. Although this might make for a noble crusade, it's a doomed one; the very nature of TQM demands teamwork.

The multiple-level aspect of the roadmap should keep the lone rangers in check. It should prevent an executive from making an improvement in isolation, perhaps increasing productivity in one area of the company but decreasing it in another. You can turn one factory into a model of efficiency and productivity, but if you can't deploy that model in other plants, you're stuck with PQM. Suboptimizing at one level can decrease performance at another level. A middle-level team may work with outside consultants to restructure a company's information system, but it may never have analyzed the requirements for the restructured system with the working-level people who use it daily. When the new system is deployed, major snafus can occur regularly. Each level must intersect with another level, and when those intersections are ignored, problems result.

The most important intersections are the ones that deploy strategic intent from the executive and middle levels to the working level. Remember, improvements rarely occur at the upper two levels. You need to deploy strategies intact, and a multiple-level perspective will help you do so.

Chapter 10 on the team structure and roles will show you how to develop a linked multilevel team structure capable of deploying strategy and policy downward and vertically and horizontally integrating all improvements. Before we do that, however, we need to examine the third face of our roadmap cube.

Chapter 5

It's Just a Phase You'll Be Going Through

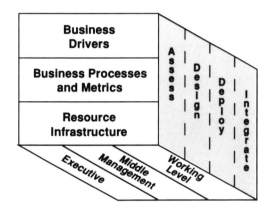

The four phases that comprise the side of our roadmap cube will be familiar to anyone who has been involved with large-scale project management. The cube is also intended to suggest a continuous recycling through the four phases. Our map's phases are somewhat akin to the four phases of the Shewart/Deming cycle, but even if the Shewart/Deming cycle or project management is new to you, the four phases should make intuitive sense. They impose a sequential logic and linkages on the improvement process, providing management with control over the objectives, timing, and costs of improvements.

Too often, that control is missing. Improvements are frequently implemented in a random fashion. The quality team meets, and agenda items from the meeting provide the only structure for improvements; planning happens at a very incremental pace. Without a systematic approach, PQM is the result.

The four phases allow you to define desired outputs at the end of each phase, organize projects around those outputs, and monitor progress on each project. Since you may have scores of projects going on simultaneously and activity taking place in different *phases* on three or more different *levels*, control is essential.

An Example of How Phases Work

The sales process/order entry example from Chapter 4 provides us with a good model for understanding the four phases. To give you a sense of what activities take place during each phase, we've constructed a sample (and incomplete) list of tasks for each phase for improving the order entry process at the working level. As you look at the list, remember that the specific tasks in each phase will be shaped by the level of activity—the tasks and outputs of the executive level are very different from those of the middle management level. If we created lists for all three levels, each would be different.

In this introduction to the phases, however, the following list should give you a general sense of what's involved.

Sales Order Entry Process Improvement: Working Levels

Tasks	*Outputs*
Phase 1: Assess	
• Customer interviews	• Customer requirements
• Sales department interviews	• As-is process maps. Improvement targets of opportunity
• Root cause analysis	• Improvement plan
Phase 2: Design	
• Establish order entry output measures	• Output measures
• Establish process, goals, and measures	• Process metrics and standards
• Remap the process	• Redesigned order entry process
• Pilot-test redesigned process	• Test results

Tasks	Outputs
Phase 3: Deploy	
• Prepare deployment plan and timetable for order entry process	• Deployment plan
• Deployment tracking and support	• Deployment results
Phase 4: Integration	
• Integration assessment of: —Manufacturing schedule —Pricing policy	• Integration requirements: —Manufacturing schedule —Pricing policy
• Integration planning	• Integration plan
• Integration work	• Integration results

While working on tasks during these phases, you have access to a wide variety of project management tools, such as:

- Project management software
- PERT charts
- Project plans per phase
- Role definition
- Resource management
- Milestone reviews
- Progress and jeopardy reports

Key Aspects of Each Phase

Keeping these lists in mind, let's discuss some of the most significant aspects of each phase.

In many ways, Phase 1 is the most important for achieving improvement goals, and also the most challenging. It requires assessment and planning using the other two faces of the cube—assessment and planning that begins on the executive level and cascades down to the middle and working levels. The executive leadership team uses the front face to search for improvement targets throughout the business—the one or two areas where the gap between the actual and the desired is biggest and where the return on an improvement investment will be greatest. Once this team has made its assessment, targeting the sales process as in our previous example, middle management can repeat these mapping activities, only this time within a process rather than a companywide context. Middle management too will identify targets of opportunity within the process based on business drivers, process and metrics, and infrastructure resources. Once it has homed in on the order entry process as the primary target, the working level maps out this particular process in great detail.

At the end of Phase 1, an epiphany occurs. Contrary to what you may have believed, you don't have to make scores of simultaneous improvements to achieve a major return on your investment. Examining a process via the cube and using Pareto analysis of your opportunities reveals the priority order of improvements that will give you the biggest bang for the buck. Because the map helps you "see" otherwise invisible connections between activities in this early stage, you can anticipate a lack of equipment, a need for training, a customer concern conflicting with government regulations, etc.—you can plan effectively so that the improvement stays on course.

Phase 2, design and testing, is straightforward. Accepted design and test methodology is fine to use, and there are scores of good books on the subject. From an improvement standpoint, the main goal of this phase is to produce a validated improvement that is ready to be deployed.

Phase 3, deployment, requires you to answer one burning question: How do we deploy a validated improvement in a variety of offices, plants, and locations?

Phase 4, integration, is probably the most neglected phase. The improvements designed, tested, and deployed in Phases 2 and 3 must be integrated with other processes and infrastructure elements. Integration can be difficult because it's like doing a jigsaw puzzle where the pieces are constantly changing shape; continuous improvement means continuous integration.

None of these phases is set in stone. In fact, milestone reviews should be conducted, at a minimum, at the end of each phase. What you learn at the end of a phase will reshape the assumptions and the plan with which you started. New or updated project plans should be created at the beginning of each new phase. All this means, of course, that the overall project plan created at the very beginning of the improvement effort must be adaptable, and must be designed to be robust enough to accommodate the anticipated changes.

Also keep in mind that the ideal chronology of the phases won't be replicated in real life. For one overall improvement, you may have 17 projects. With each project going through four phases with some at different levels, you're bound to have one project completed before another. While one project is in the design and test phase, another may be working through integration issues. Good project management and concomitant mapping are the only things that will help you control this syncopated activity.

Shortcuts and Penalties

You may be tempted to skip a phase or move through it with careless speed, pushing hard toward your improvement goal. Although certain paths will help you reach quality faster than others, there are no easy shortcuts. Each phase is essential and linked to the others—treat one with disrespect, and you diminish all of them. Here are some common shortcuts to avoid and the penalties you'll receive if you take them anyway.

Phase 1—Poor improvement opportunity analysis. Some organizations fail to do the comprehensive, comparative analysis of improvement possibilities that Phase 1 demands. Sometimes they pick the wrong targets—targets that have relatively poor ROI. Other times, they decide to improve everything at once, which is a sure path to frustration. Shooting from the hip is a common American habit, and when we act before we analyze, we end up with a collection of improvements that waste resources and don't add up to better business performance—you may improve a process, but that improvement may cause ten other problems downstream and really cause an overall suboptimization. Analysis provides you with a baseline for measuring improvements. If you lack that baseline, you can't determine the success of an improvement with any degree of accuracy. People often claim to have made great improvements ("We really have a better order entry process now"), but compared to what? Is the process better than domestic competitors'? Foreign competitors'? Is it better in terms of speed? In terms of increased revenues? What other "costs" will this improvement really incur, and what ROI is really achievable? The analysis that goes with Phase 1 ensures that these questions are answered.

Phase 2—No pilot test. What happens when you skip from Phase 1 to Phase 3 with no stop for testing in between? Here are three possibilities.

1. You deploy an improvement and have to make expensive and time-consuming fixes in multiple locations rather than in one test location.

2. People who receive the flawed, deployed improvement turn against management and its "harebrained quality schemes." This is what gives TQM a bad name. Testing helps prevent these negative attitudes.
3. You miss a problematic situation caused by the improvement. For instance, you have an improvement for the order entry process. While you're deploying the improvement, productivity dips—everyone is on the learning curve and getting used to the new system, and initially the new process doesn't work as fast as the old one. Orders pile up, and customers complain. If this problem is spotted in a pilot test, you can prepare for it by adding temporary personnel or paying overtime to compensate for the anticipated lost productivity or doing a better job of initial training to support the change.

Phase 3—Not deploying at all or deploying without customizing. The former shortcut means that you confine an improvement to one plant or location for financial or other reasons. The improvement that tested so well in Phase 2 doesn't achieve its full potential impact. The latter problem—deploying without customizing—is the more common short-cut. Organizations try to force-fit improvements, failing to accommodate different volumes, customer bases, and employee skills. Deploying properly means deploying flexibly, tailoring an improvement to the specific traits and needs of each group.

Phase 4—No integration or a Band-Aid approach. This is where many quality efforts reach a dead end. Instead of making the effort to reshape the organization to deal with changes wrought by improvements, you either ignore the changes or make token efforts. The classic information system Band-Aid: "I know the new system is causing a headache for everyone, but for now, we'll just manually reenter data into the computer and work out the bugs later." What really happens is that everyone learns to tolerate an imperfect system instead of fixing it. Instead of working out the bugs immediately and integrating the system into the organization, a Band-Aid is slapped on. The penalty here, of course, is a jury-rigged improvement that may fall apart because it isn't sustainable in the total process and infrastructure environment.

Gaining Control

For many executives, quality and project management may seem like strange bedfellows. Project management is often thought of as confined to the engineering/manufacturing arena; it may seem odd to apply it to TQM. But this is absolutely essential if you want control over improvements. Project management sets up a planning, action, and reporting cycle that helps you direct and keep track of results and resources. For any executive who has experienced the helpless feeling that often accompanies PQM, such control is a gift.

As you'll see in the next four chapters, the phases help you define all your projects in relation to one another as well as to the whole program, enabling you to identify the specific tasks, the sequence of activities, and the dependency of activities (one activity can't proceed until another one is completed, for instance). While the four phases help you coordinate your improvement efforts, they also give you a sense of what has to be done to achieve your improvement goals.

This minimizes the likelihood of surprises such as unexpected delays, shortfalls of resources, and many other potential roadblocks. Now let's look at Phase 1 in greater detail.

Chapter 6

Phase 1: Where Are You Now, Where Do You Want to Go?

More than any other chapter in the book, this one will be filled with maps. That's because more than any other phase, this is the one where it's easiest to lose your way. Unless you analyze and plan your improvements with the holistic, linked framework a roadmap provides, you'll slip into PQM.

Although some of these charts and the methods of creating them will be familiar, the analytical approach to improvements may be quite different. The process of attaining quality can seem magical and mysterious. Though theorists talk a lot about quality and organizations promote their improvements, TQM remains a rather vague methodology. The step-by-step road that leads to quality is invisible to most organizations that are on the outside looking in.

This phase and the maps contained here make it visible. You'll learn how they can focus your efforts on the right improvement targets and help you make improvements that facilitate rather than frustrate your business strategy. Let's begin with a view of the typical purposes and outputs for the three levels in Phase 1—"master map," shown in Exhibit 6-1.

Setting Forth the Ground Rules

This is the master map for the assessment and planning phase. In general terms, it suggests the purposes and outputs for each of the three levels during Phase 1. Although much more detailed maps must follow, this introductory map accomplishes a number of objectives.

Exhibit 6-1.   Master map from Phase 1 for each level.

Executive Level

<u>Phase 1</u>

Purpose: **Provide strategic direction for the business-wide improvement**
program

<u>Outputs</u>

- **Business Architecture**
  - **Business drivers**
  - **Business processes and metrics**
  - **Resource infrastructure**

- **Strategic Assessment**
  - **All areas of the business architecture assessment**
  - **Strategic targets of opportunity prioritized**

- **Improvement Strategic Plan**
  - **Vision, strategies, values**
  - **Team structure**
  - **Improvement goals and timeline**
  - **Improvement investment plan**
  - **TQM infrastructure and processes**

Middle Management Level

<u>Phase 1</u>

Purpose: **Provide strategic direction for the improvement program within**
the scope of a middle management improvement team and the
companywide improvement strategy

<u>Outputs</u>

- **Business Architecture (within team scope)**

- **Assessment Results**

- **Prioritized Targets of Opportunity**

- **Improvement Plans**
  - **Long-term strategy**
  - **Improvement goals and timeline**
  - **Short-term program plan and budget**
  - **Subordinate team structure**

(continues)

Exhibit 6-1.   Continued

Working Level

<u>Phase 1</u>

Purpose: Provide direction and focus to working-level improvement projects

<u>Outputs</u>

- Customers/Stakeholders and Their Requirements

- As-is Process Maps

- Infrastructure Description

- Prioritized Targets of Opportunity

- Improvement Plan and Budget

First, it involves all organizational levels in a sequential, connected manner. In many improvement efforts, you'll find numerous process maps at the working level, but few or none at the middle management and executive levels. Going "mapless" virtually ensures a lack of linkages from the top down—the working-level teams will be moving forward with little input from or coordination with other levels. As you can see from this map, the assessment and planning activities cascade down. If you examine the outputs for Phase 1 for each level, you'll also see the cascading connections: The executive level maps the front face of the cube, the middle management level maps the face for its particular process, and the working level creates detailed "as-is" process maps. The point: There are no dangling teams or random activity, since everyone's outputs are related to the whole.

Second, this master map ensures that business strategy is guiding improvement projects. Quality for quality's sake has been rightly attacked by the media and corporate leaders. Yet it's all too easy to embark on an improvement program that is unrelated to major business goals. Everyone gets so caught up in the spirit of quality that they neglect the salient business issues. The maps here focus all levels on those issues. The executive-level purpose is: "Provide *strategic* direction for the businesswide improvement program." The middle management–level purpose: "Provide *strategic* direction for the improvement program within . . . *the companywide improvement strategy.*" The outputs, too, reflect this strategic business emphasis. Again, this flows down to the working-level teams, who possess the direction necessary to avoid nonstrategic water cooler projects.

Third, assessment drives planning for all phases, enabling an organization to anticipate obstacles and other issues that may emerge down the road. Not only can you anticipate these issues, you can plan to do something about them right from the start. For example, the integration phase is frequently ignored. No thought is given and no plan is created for readjustments caused by an improvement. No one looks into the future and determines whether the information system is compatible with a proposed improvement in the marketing process, or whether new people with specific skills must be recruited to facilitate an improvement in manufacturing. Tackling these potential problems at the start greatly increases the odds against disconnects between processes. No doubt, your Phase 1 map will change as you actually move through the four phases. Experience will allow you to make midcourse corrections, so don't think your first map will be your last one.

Now let's look at how the executive-level Phase 1 map unfolds into a sequence of output maps.

From Business Strategy to Team Structure

Mapping the front face of the cube is an essential executive-level task in this phase. The business drivers shown in Exhibit 6-2 are the result of the executive leadership committee's analysis of the company's assets and competencies, stakeholder requirements, and marketplace and competitive factors. Although this may be a relatively easy step, it's important to be thorough—the stakeholder requirements listed here, for instance, must include more than the customer.

Mapping the middle section of the cube, as in Exhibit 6-3, should be a familiar task by now. Notice, however, that TQM appears as a box within the leadership processes and not within the support processes (where some organizations might be tempted to put it).

The missing puzzle piece in many improvement programs is that shown in Exhibit 6-4. When the measurement hierarchy is missing, improvements fail to meet business objectives. It stands to reason that if an improvement strategy isn't designed to satisfy key business measurement criteria, it's doubtful that the actual improvement will satisfy them. Similarly, if you don't break each business measure down into its component parts and determine where it ranks in the hierarchy (in percentage terms), an improvement may satisfy only a relatively low-

(Text continues on page 67)

Exhibit 6-2. Business drivers.

Assets/Competencies	Stakeholder Requirements	Marketplace and Competitive Factors
• Integrated information system linked to customer information system • Fast-response product development • Deep pockets • Metalworking technology leadership	• Customers – Design cycle time – Price – JIT delivery – Controlled quality • Owners – ROI – Equity growth • Employees – Secure employment – Competitive income – Job satisfaction • Regulatory – EPA – OSHA – EEO	• Overcapacity in a mature market • Major customers reducing number of suppliers and forming close partnership with survivors. • Survivors must be prepared to grow and to drive down cost, provide JIT inventory, and provide statistical process control data

Exhibit 6-3. Business processes.

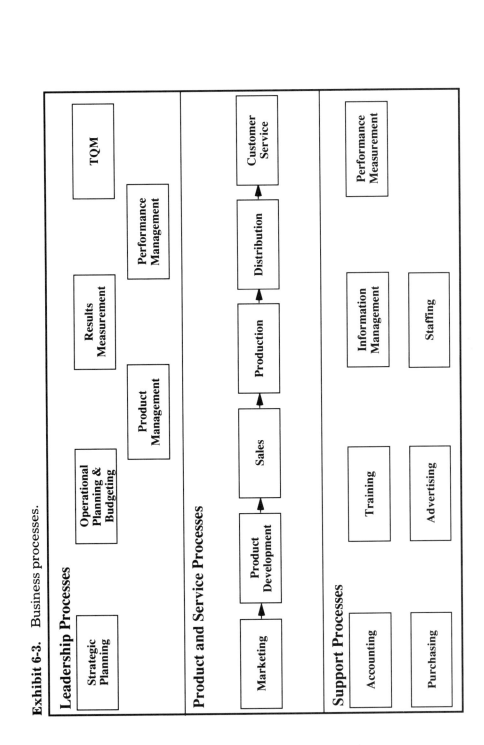

Leadership Processes

Strategic Planning	Operational Planning & Budgeting	Results Measurement	TQM

Product Management	Performance Management

Product and Service Processes

Marketing → Product Development → Sales → Production → Distribution → Customer Service

Support Processes

Accounting	Training	Information Management	Performance Measurement

Purchasing	Advertising	Staffing

Exhibit 6-4. The business measurement hierarchy.

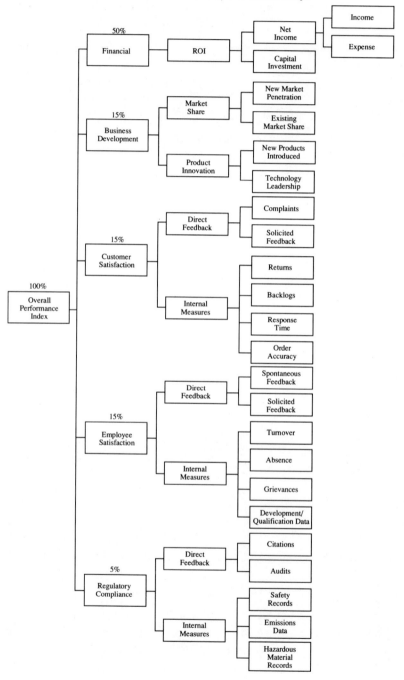

priority measure or may neglect a key aspect of a measure (focusing only on market share and ignoring product innovation, for example). Finally, remember that your measurement hierarchy is not limited to financials. Though at times financial performance may seem to be the be-all and end-all of the business, this sample hierarchy shows only half the total weight being given to financial performance.

Beginning work on improvements without a thorough analysis of your infrastructure invites disaster. It's not unusual for an organization to invest a great deal of time and money on improving a process, only to discover that it lacks essential resources to make that improvement happen. Exhibit 6-5 breaks the infrastructure into environmental and human resources. It's not enough to quantify these resources. You also have to determine what and where your critical competencies are, and evaluate the total scope of your environmental resources, from organization structure to consequences.

Strategic goals flow from the vision (Exhibit 6-6). Typically, executives suggest scores of goals. Try to focus on the six or seven that, if they are achieved, will actualize the vision.

Here's a simple, effective technique for prioritizing improvement targets. List five such targets, then evaluate them based on their impact on business performance measures, as shown in Exhibit 6-7. A high impact receives three points, a medium impact two points, and a low impact one point. Multiply each point value by the weighting for the business measure. For instance, a high impact (3 points) for target 1 multiplied by .50 equals 1.50. Add the adjusted points for all four measures, and see if the sum for that target is greater or less than the sums for the other opportunity targets. The highest one is your primary target—the place where the improvement will mean the most to your business. This example may seem simplistic. You can use much more sophisticated comparison methods, but we're aware of major corporations that are launching major change efforts with no comparative evaluation at all.

Analyzing your organization's values, Exhibit 6-8, may seem like a "soft and fuzzy" assessment compared to the more tangible activities of Phase 1. But unless you know your company's values and determine whether they're congruent with your improvements, those values can turn into an impediment. For instance, if one of your company's values is fierce internal competition, teamwork will be a difficult goal to attain. In Exhibit 6-8, you'll find values consistent with improvement goals.

You need to create two views of your team structure: the ultimate and the start-up. The double-outlined boxes in Exhibit 6-9 designate

(Text continues on page 71)

Exhibit 6-5. Infrastructure: environmental and human resources.

Organization Structure	Information	Facilities	Tools & Equipment	Materials	Consequences
• Organization Structure Chart • Departmental Roles/ Responsibilities Descriptions • Job Descriptions • Team Structure • Team Charters	• Financial Database • Human Resource Database • MRPII • Customer Database • Supplier Database • Procedure and Policy Manuals	• 2 Plants • Headquarters Office • 6 Regional Sales Offices • 8 Warehouses	• Production Machinery • Hand Tools • Power Tools • Material Handling Machinery • Automated Controls • Vehicles • Computers • Workstations • Communications Network	• Raw Materials • Supplies	• Profit Sharing Plan • Executive Bonus Plan • Performance Management System

Infrastructure

Human Resources

Total Work Force = 6250		Locations		
Functions	**HQ Office**	**Plant 1**	**Plant 2**	**Regional Offices**
• **General Management**				
- **Executives**	26			
- **Support**	50			
• **Production**				
- **Management**	1	25	36	
- **Hourly**	1	2522	3343	
- **Technical Support**		36	39	
- **Engineering**	1	12	15	
• **Sales**				
- **Management**	1			14
- **Sales Representatives**				121
- **Support**	1			53
• **Research and Development**				
- **Management**	3			
- **Engineering**	5			
- **Technical Support**	6			

(continues)

Exhibit 6-5. Continued

Infrastructure

Functions	Critical Competencies				
	Metal-working	Information Management	Cost Control Strategies	Integrated Prod. Dev.	Integrated Operations
General Management					
- Executives		X	X	X	X
- Support		X			
Production					
- Management	X	X	X	X	X
- Hourly	X				
- Technical Support	X				X
- Engineering	X		X	X	X
Sales					
- Management		X	X	X	X
- Sales Representatives					X
- Support			X		
Research and Development					
- Management	X	X	X	X	
- Engineering	X	X	X	X	
- Technical Support	X			X	

Exhibit 6-6. Vision and strategic goals.

Vision

- **Survive the fallout in the industry**

- **Grow the business to three times its present size**

- **Become an industry leader in low-cost, high-quality production**

- **Achieve fully integrated operations and information**

- **Achieve rapid product development**

- **Achieve steady growth of net income and owners' equity**

- **Be recognized as a preferred employer**

Strategic Goals

- **Define and improve the sales process**

- **Integrate and optimize operations cost and cycle time**

- **Create an integrated product development process**

- **Establish a customer satisfaction measurement system**

- **Develop strategies and tactics to improve employee relations**

start-up teams that must be established initially—they correspond to the targets of opportunity prioritized in Exhibit 6-7. Similarly, you'll establish supporting project teams: customer satisfaction measurement, operations optimization, and employee relations. These are task force teams, whose existence begins and ends with an assigned project. Unlike the other teams on the map, they are temporary. Be sure to map all the teams here, not just the permanent ones. Even though some of them won't exist at first, mapping them provides a framework with which to view the team structure.

The map for sales process improvement goals in Exhibit 6-10 is only one of many such maps you should have—there should be one for each corresponding process. Created by the executive leadership team, these

Exhibit 6-7. Strategic targets of opportunity.

Priority	Strategies	Points	Impact on Business Performance Measures (Weight)					
			50% Financial	15% Business Development	15% Customer Satisfaction	15% Employee Satisfaction	5% Regulatory Compliance	
1	Integrate and optimize operations cost and cycle time	2.45	H	H	M	L	L	
2	Define and improve the sales process	1.95	H	M	L	—	—	
3	Create an integrated product development process	1.90	M	H	M	L	—	
4	Establish a customer satisfaction measurement system	1.40	L	M	H	L	—	
5	Develop strategies and tactics to improve employee relations	1.25	L	—	M	H	—	

Note: Multiply high, medium, and low values by weights = points

Value: H = 3 points, M = 2 points, L = 1 point

Exhibit 6-8. Organization values.

• **External competition, internal teamwork**
• **Open partnerships with customers and suppliers**
• **Recognize the importance of employee contribution and support employees with development, recognition, and necessary resources**
• **Continuous improvement**
• **Synergy through diversity**
• **Safety first**

goals are part of the team chartering process. Rather than simply launching an improvement team like a rudderless boat, we're suggesting that clear and prioritized goals be provided to that team.

Goals aren't the only things that improvement teams should be given. Deliverables and timetables like those shown in Exhibit 6-11 help ensure accountability. In Phase 1, you have the opportunity to communicate expectations to teams, decreasing the likelihood of misunderstandings down the road. You don't have to map out all the deliverables and dates for each phase now. In this example, only the first two phases have been charted.

There are all types of methods of budgeting for improvements; you certainly don't have to follow the one in Exhibit 6-12. The important thing is to chart your expected resource expenditures for targeted improvements for this year and next.

Without a support structure planned for and in place, your improvement efforts can crumble in Phase 2, 3, or 4. Create a map, from the executive leadership on down, of the people who will provide crucial support for improvement activities. Two common, overlooked support groups are coordinators and facilitators. The map in Exhibit 6-13 shows how coordinators and facilitators are linked to the leadership team and the TQM director. More on this support structure and roles appears in Chapter 11.

The final executive-level map, shown in Exhibit 6-14, is an expanded view of the TQM process itself. The TQM process is divided into leadership, product and services, and support subprocesses. The product and services improvement processes mirror the four phases, and

Exhibit 6-9. Team structure.

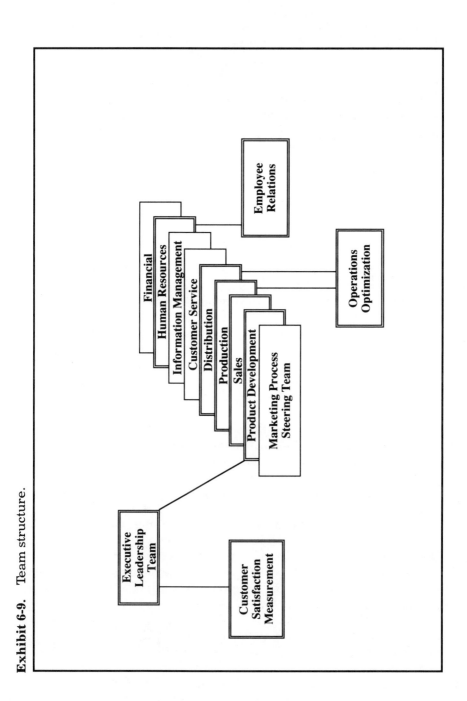

Exhibit 6-10. Sales process improvement goals.

1. **Analyze market segments and develop sales strategies for each segment**

2. **Define an improved sales process**

3. **Establish a clear sales measurement system linked to business measurement hierarchy**

4. **Develop recommendations for tactical improvements (e.g., sales teams, organization, job definition, information)**

the leadership and support processes guide and support the improvement projects in the middle.

Mapping of the middle and working levels in Phase 1 roughly follows what we've done for the executive level. Rather than repeating the same mapping exercises for these other two levels, we've given two samples of each, focusing on the sales process; this should give you a sense of the variations that come with each level. For the middle management level, the first sales process map, Exhibit 6-15, corresponds to the middle slice of the front face of the cube. As you can see, the three types of processes are charted as they relate to sales. The second map, Exhibit 6-16, completes the middle slice with a flowchart of the sales measurement hierarchy.

Coming down to the working level, Exhibits 6-17 and 6-18 take a targeted subprocess, order entry, and break it down into details crucial for improvements. Exhibit 6-17 traces the routes an order can take as it enters, flows through, and exits from the order entry system. Exhibit 6-18 lists very specific customer satisfaction and financial measures for this subprocess.

A Change Machine

When organizations complete Phase 1, they are astonished by the complexity of the structure they produce and the amount of work that structure tells them they'll be doing in the ensuing phases. At the same time, however, they understand how all this work will result in a real strategic improvement. All these maps make visible the invisible road

(Text continues on page 83)

Exhibit 6-11. Sales process improvement project deliverables and timetable.

Milestone Dates

Phase 1:

- **Project Plan**   **February 1, Year 1**
- **Market Segment Analysis**   **April 1, Year 1**
- **As-is Sales Process Map**   **April 1, Year 1**
- **Improvement opportunity list**   **May 1, Year 1**
  and priorities

Phase 2:

- **Project Plan**   **June 1, Year 1**
- **Sales Strategies**   **July 1, Year 1**
- **New Sales Process Map**   **August 1, Year 1**
- **Sales Measurement System**   **September 1, Year 1**
  Design and Test Results
- **Other sub-projects resulting**   **Per Project Plan**
  from Phase 1 analysis

Phase 3:   **To be determined after Phase 1**
                                                  and updated after Phase 2

Phase 4:   **To be determined after Phase 1**
                                                  and updated after Phase 2

Exhibit 6-12. Improvement investment plan.

Project	Year 1 $(000)	Year 2 $(000)
1. Operations Optimization	500	300
2. Sales Process Improvement	150	250
3. Integrated Product Development	60	50
4. Customer Satisfaction Measurement	50	40
5. Employee Relations	50	20
6. Other		240
7. TQM Leadership and Support	100	100
Total	910	1,000

Exhibit 6-13. TQM support structure.

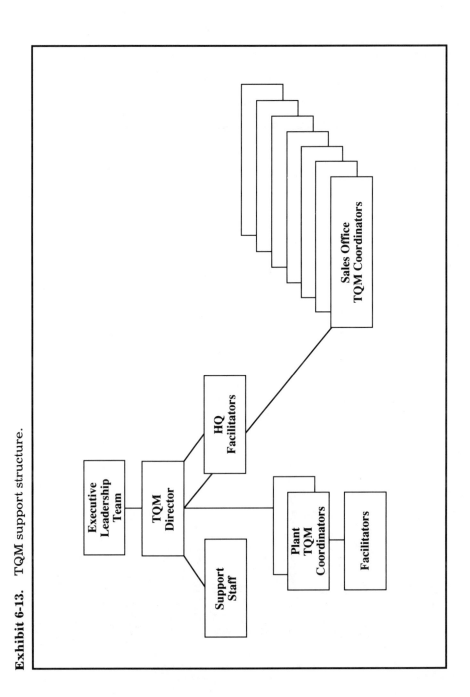

Exhibit 6-14. Expanded view of the TQM process.

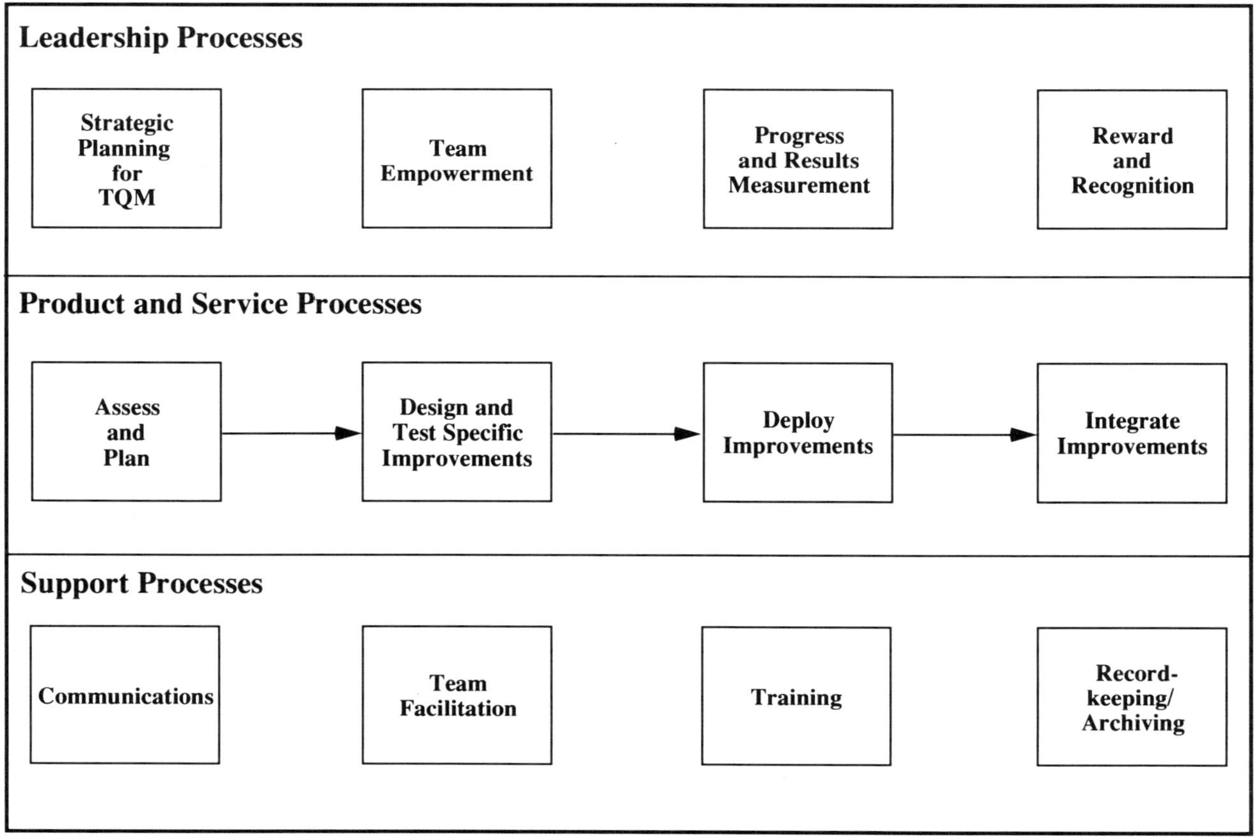

Leadership Processes

| Strategic Planning for TQM | Team Empowerment | Progress and Results Measurement | Reward and Recognition |

Product and Service Processes

Assess and Plan → Design and Test Specific Improvements → Deploy Improvements → Integrate Improvements

Support Processes

| Communications | Team Facilitation | Training | Record-keeping/Archiving |

Exhibit 6-15. Sales process map (middle management level).

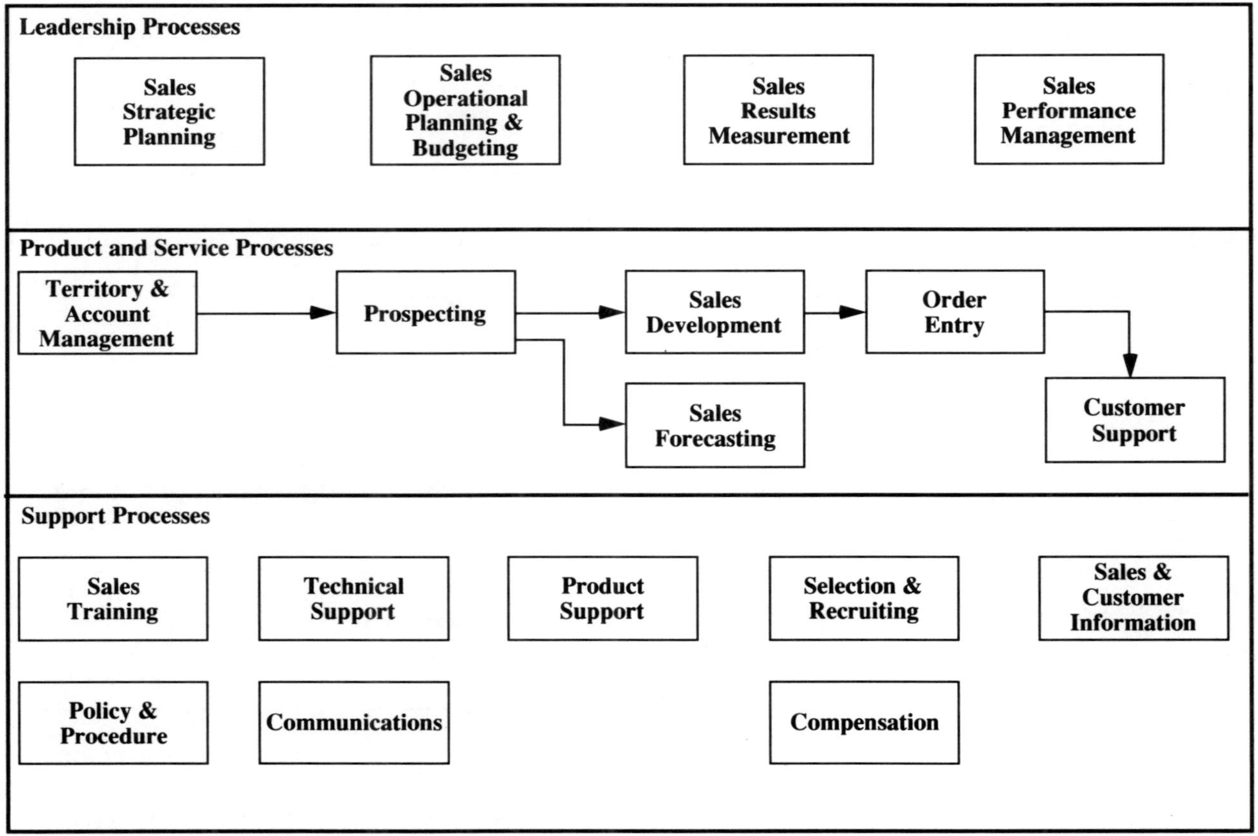

Leadership Processes

| Sales Strategic Planning | Sales Operational Planning & Budgeting | Sales Results Measurement | Sales Performance Management |

Product and Service Processes

Territory & Account Management → Prospecting → Sales Development → Order Entry → Customer Support

Prospecting → Sales Forecasting

Sales Development → Order Entry

Support Processes

| Sales Training | Technical Support | Product Support | Selection & Recruiting | Sales & Customer Information |
| Policy & Procedure | Communications | | Compensation | |

Exhibit 6-16. Sales measurement hierarchy (middle management level). (Financial Only)

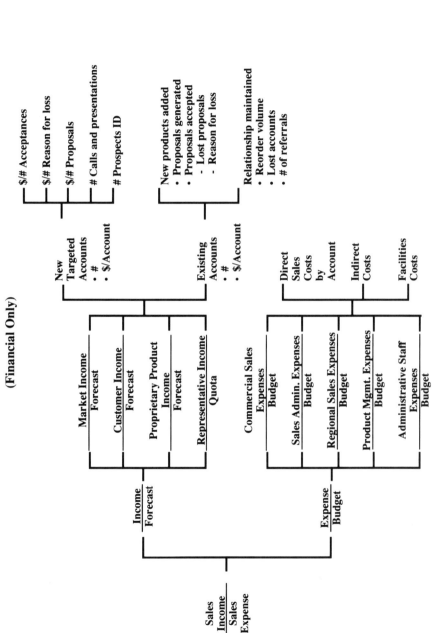

Exhibit 6-17. Sales order entry routes (working level).

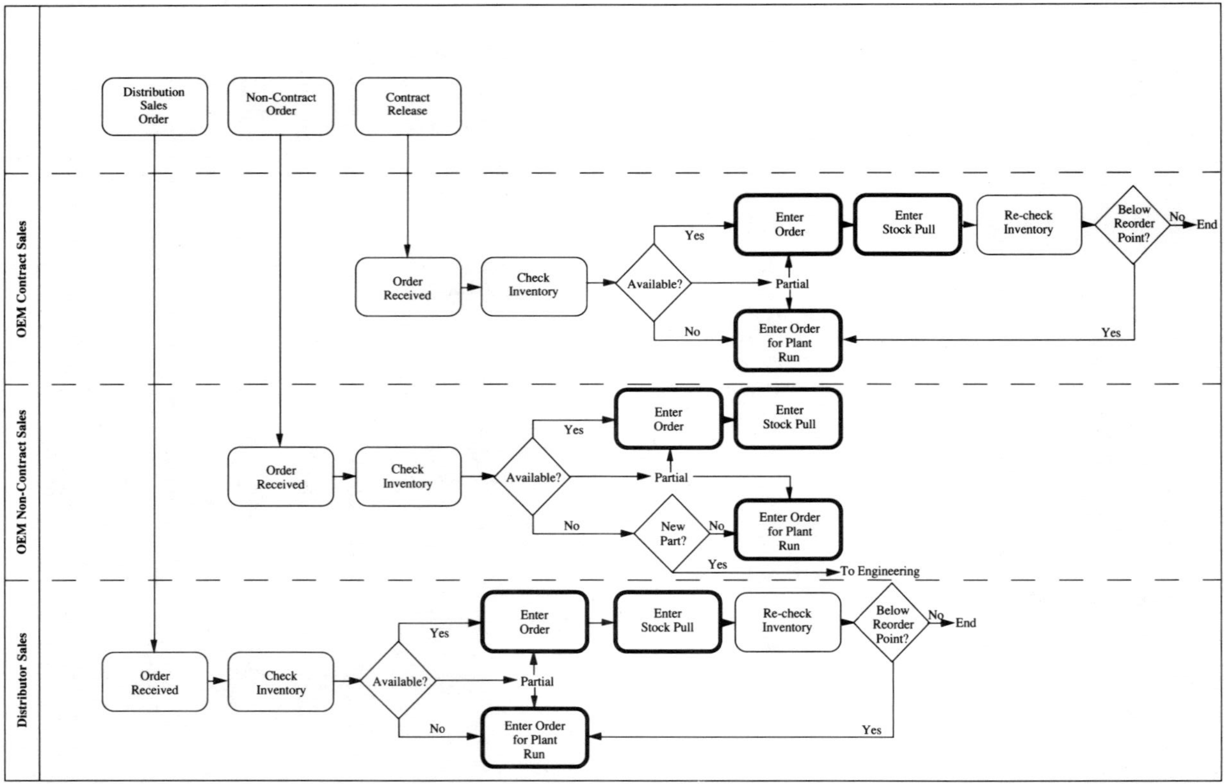

Exhibit 6-18. Sales order entry measures (working level).

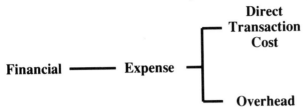

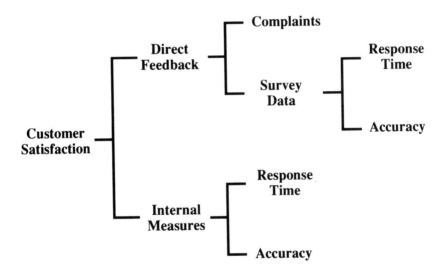

that leads to quality. As you assess and plan at different organizational levels, you begin to see how seemingly unrelated activities are intimately connected—how the business measurement hierarchy affects the choice and ranking of improvement opportunities, for instance.

One of our clients wanted to make an improvement in operations, but when it completed Phase 1, it realized that it couldn't make that improvement unless other "connected" processes were taken into consideration. In the past, this company had produced significant amounts of "safety" stock to ensure that customer orders could always be filled quickly. But the operations improvement required the company to drive costs down by driving inventory levels down. When the company mapped this improvement during Phase 1, the connection with sales forecasting appeared almost magically. If inventory levels were to decrease dramatically, sales forecasting accuracy had to increase dramatically. Although some of these internal customer interconnections might seem obvious, most aren't. They're buried in the functional silos that define American business, where the sales forecasting people are effectively segregated from the operations staff.

As you review the charts from Phase 1, we think you'll understand how these silos can be penetrated horizontally. There is no place in the cube for functional analysis. Everything is viewed through the lens of process. The sales process does not equal the Sales Department. This is especially valuable for middle managers, who tend to be most burdened with silo mindsets. During this first phase, their role in the process is clearly defined—their support and coordination are absolutely essential. When middle managers don't feel left out, they don't sabotage improvements.

The executive level, too, experiences a similar change in mindset. We know of one CEO who, when we explained that the executive leadership group was going to have to spend a great deal of time together during Phase 1, said, "We've never spent more than two hours together at one time in the past three years."

We've found that it's difficult for top executives to work together intensively because they often don't view the business holistically—the concept of the internal customer escapes them. They often don't understand anything about how they must work together as a team to define and optimize overall performance. But once the Phase 1 maps begin taking shape, the possibilities for executive teamwork become clear. As inputs and outputs for each process are mapped, executives can trace with their fingers the flow of activities from their domain to another. When they grasp the concept of one process serving another and major processes crossing organizational boundaries, they become much more willing to work together.

Another incentive for executives to work together is the chance to implement change. In company after company, executives labor for months to design strategies and goals to reshape the business. Yet those strategies and goals, as good and as right as they might be, too often lead nowhere because the machinery needed to bring all their ideas to fruition is missing.

Phase 1 creates the machinery they've been looking for. It helps create a plan and machinery for turning hard-core business strategies into real-life improvements.

There's no substitute for this type of thorough analysis and planning. Yet substitutes abound, especially when organizations treat quality improvement as a separate program or a training and internal public relations campaign. Typically, when the improvement process stalls, an organization seizes on one or even all of the following substitute suggestions from those inside and outside:

- We need more leadership that can communicate our vision and goals throughout the organization. Once we train people in leadership and interpersonal skills, we'll get the improvements back on track.
- We need more teams and projects; once we have them, we'll get the momentum back.
- We need to spread the quality religion at all levels of the organization, so let's send our people to quality colleges, and when they come back, they'll be ready to help us move forward.

Each of the above is an example of PQM. Substitutes are only partial solutions. TQM requires far more. The defining moment of Phase 1 is when you glimpse the holistic aspect of making improvements. It may happen not while you're mapping the nitty-gritty details, but after you've completed some of your maps and have had a chance to look at others' contributions to them. When you see the sequence of improvement activities, the connections between people and processes, and the way business strategy selects improvement opportunities, you will realize that you can finally plan major changes that will actually be tested, deployed, and integrated into the organization. That's quality, not for quality's sake, but for the sake of the business.

Chapter 7

Road Test

You've emerged from Phase 1 with some critical outputs: targeted improvements, projects with macro plans developed to make those improvements happen, teams identified for formal setup and chartering to work on those projects. Armed with the maps created in the first phase, you can journey through the next three phases, which revolve around project work. Since scores or even hundreds of projects will be launched, you shouldn't expect all projects to proceed at the same speed—one project may necessarily spend a longer time in Phase 2 while another project is planned to zip along through to Phase 4.

In this chapter, we're concerned with *Phase 2, design and test*, project activities. We'll take you through the sequence of activities that will increase the speed and smoothness with which you progress through this phase.

Getting Started

Design and test start-up activities include:

- Establishing a sponsor and chartering a team for the project
- Team orientation and training
- Team development of its own project plan

Chartering a team should be a formal (written) process. If it is done informally, projects lack the clarity required for necessary organization and accountability. Therefore, create a document to charter your team that addresses the following issues:

- What is the purpose of the project—what specifically is it intended to achieve?
- What are the success metrics—how will success be measured?

- Who are full- and part-time members of the project team, and what are their specific roles and responsibilities?
- Who is the sponsor and who are the other key stakeholders?
- What other people are key resources of the team (even if they're not full-time members)?
- What are the deliverables and milestone dates—what specific things should be produced by the team by what dates?
- What are the terms of empowerment and the limits of empowerment?

Most of this list is self-explanatory. The last item, however, causes some confusion. Empowerment is not a blank check you give to a team. Limits must be set. For instance, a team may be empowered to spend so many dollars on a project, but can't exceed that amount without permission of the executive leadership team; or the charter may designate what resources the team has access to, but also prohibits it from using other resources (such as a marketing plan that has to be kept classified for competitive reasons).

Once the charter is written, an initial team meeting is scheduled at which team members evaluate it. The team has the opportunity to negotiate certain aspects of the charter with the leadership team. In many instances, negotiation involves the scope of the project (team members may find it too broad or too narrow) and time (team members may feel that their daily job responsibilities will make it difficult for them to accomplish project tasks within the targeted timeframes). The sample charter in Exhibit 7-1 will give you a sense of how it should look.

Orientation and Training

Some teams will be unfamiliar with the four-phase process, project planning, or even the organization's overall TQM approach. Training in each of these areas should be made available to team members before Phase 2 design and testing work begins. Similarly, team members should be informed about the spectrum of quality improvement tools available to them. Though training in the use of these tools isn't necessary at the outset, team members should be aware that the tools exist so that they can incorporate them into project work when needed. For instance, a team might require statistical design of experiments. The team should understand what the tool does and what internal consultant resources it might employ within the project. At the point when it

(Text continues on page 92)

Exhibit 7-1.   Sample team charter.

TQM Team Charter

Team: *Sales/Marketing Processes*
Purpose/Mission: *To improve the performance of Company Q marketing and sales processes*
Scope: *Sales, Marketing, and Pricing processes* *Marketing Database and Customer Database*
Sponsor: *Susan Black, Marketing Vice President*
Team Leader: *Steve Smith, National Sales Manager*
Facilitator: *Ed Mains*
Membership: *Harvey Jones, Marketing Director* *Ellen Jamison, National Account Manager* *Rita Gomez, Field Sales Manager* *Dan Wolfson, Market Research Director* *Gary Alderman, Product Manager* *Karin Youngquist, Sales Measurement Manager* *James Einstein, R&D Director (part-time)* *George Krump, Production Manager (part-time)*

Goals/Expectations

Goals:

1. *Define/map the existing sales, marketing, and pricing strategies and processes.*
2. *Define process performance measures and baseline present performance.*
3. *Make an assessment of opportunities to improve process performance.*
4. *Prioritize improvement opportunities.*
5. *Develop long range and short range improvement plans.*
6. *Design and test improvements.*
7. *Develop implementation plan and oversee implementation.*
8. *Assess integration issues and recommend changes to other processes and systems if needed.*

Expectations:

1. *Follow four phase improvement process cycle*
   - *Assess/Plan*
   - *Design/Test*
   - *Deploy/Implement*
   - *Integrate*
2. *Develop and document project plans for each phase.*
3. *Prepare a report at the end of each phase.*
4. *Submit plans and reports for Executive Leadership Team review and archives.*
5. *Use good project management practices and tools.*

Deliverables   ### Dates

- *Marketing improvement strategy linked to business vision*

- *Sales improvement strategy linked to marketing strategy*

- *Marketing process and roles*

- *Sales process and roles*

- *Performance Measurement Plan*   *7/31/93*

- *Tactical Plan for Marketing and Sales improvements*

(continues)

Exhibit 7-1.   Continued

Important Coordination Links	
Teams	**Departments**
• *Strategic Planning* • *Computer Systems* • *Executive Leadership Team*	• *R&D* • *Production* • *Customer Service* • *Invoicing*
Systems/Processes	**Individuals**
• *Marketing Database* • *Customer Database* • *Results Measurement Process*	• *Division General Manager* • *Marketing and Sales Vice Presidents*

Empowerment and Limits

Time: *May expend up to five days per month per team member; more time requires Sponsor approval.*

Team Expenses: *May spend up to $50,000 in 1993; more*
(Training, Experts, Etc.)   *requires Sponsor approval.*

Access: *Open access to all Company Q officers, staff, records and information.*

Making Change:

- *Marketing and Sales Improvement Strategies and Tactical Plans must be reviewed by the Executive Leadership Team before implementation.*

- *Control over specific changes will be established after the strategies and tactical plans are approved.*

Other:

- *May establish sub-teams and include others, but must formally charter and empower them.*

- *External benchmarking is encouraged, but any sharing of Company Q information with competitors requires Sponsor approval.*

needs that tool, the appropriate number of team members should receive training in how to use it.

Developing a Project Plan

The "how-to-do-it" aspect of Phase 2 begins with a detailed project plan. Some organizations make the mistake of substituting informal lists of action items from meetings for formal project plans. The result: Crucial tasks such as proper allocation of resources and milestone reviews are easily overlooked. With proper training and/or a facilitator, any team can create a detailed project plan. Next, the team should design and develop an improvement aimed at the opportunity target. The improvement is then pilot-tested in some part of the company. From this pilot-test activity, you determine what worked and what didn't, what debugs and changes you might make in the improvement before you deploy it in the next phase. Also, you'll want to pay special attention to any downstream integration issues here. It is far better to deal with any known "disconnects" in the processes and infrastructure discovered in the pilot test now rather than after the improvement has been deployed elsewhere.

Three Levels of Projects

Project work takes place at all levels of an organization, not just at the working level. More than once, executives have expressed surprise at this fact, having trouble picturing themselves as part of an improvement team. Similarly, they're surprised to learn that improvements aren't limited to product and service processes. As you'll see, improvement projects can be located virtually anywhere on the front face of the cube, not just in the business processes slice. Let's broadly look at three typical projects, each at a different location on the front face of the cube and occurring at a different level.

Executive-Level Project

A team of top executives is created to establish a customer satisfaction measurement system. In the past, this company lacked a formal system, relying on informal reviews of customer complaints and customer service data. This project can be located in the business drivers segment of the cube—customers represent one set of business drivers, and since the executive level owns these drivers, it's in the best position to specify the measurement system in order to improve activities related to customers. The team, composed of executive leadership team members and other executives, may recruit an internal or external consultant to help it create a measurement system plan. It then maps out a project plan and creates a steering team to work with the consultant. As part of the project, the team itself might conduct surveys of existing customers to identify the key customer satisfiers and dissatisfiers. It may hear more than it wanted to about satisfaction issues such as pricing and contact protocols. The team then oversees the design of formal methods and techniques to get continuous information—surveys, telemarketing, salespeople gathering data from customers, and so on. Then a pilot test of the method is launched, and the team analyzes the results and determines whether revisions need to be made before full deployment.

Middle Management–Level Project

In this example, the focus is on the business processes slice of the cube. The middle management team is directed to set up a project to optimize production across three major connected areas: production scheduling, manufacturing, and distribution. The goal is to optimize process cycle time and reduce product costs. The reason all three areas are targeted, not just manufacturing, is that during Phase 1 it was determined that each of the three areas was optimizing its own performance at the expense of the whole (for example, by building an excessive amount of safety stock in distribution inventory).

The middle management team, therefore, must include the heads of the three functional areas, who will work together to drive down costs and cycle time. When the team meets, it might decide that mapping has to focus on the major steps of the process. The process map is created, data on cycle time and costs are collected, and the processes and interfaces between them are redesigned. Once the team is satisfied that the paper redesign is solid, it implements a pilot test in one plant, assessing the results to determine the gains in cycle time and costs. It is probable that the people who conducted the pilot test in the plant will have additional suggestions that may be incorporated into the redesigned processes before the new design is deployed in other plants.

Working-Level Project

Previously, during Phase 1, the executives determined that sales skills and product training were improvement targets with an attractive

ROI potential. Again, the location of this target on the cube is different from those of the previous two examples. Here we find it initially focused in the resource infrastructure area. The team's work begins with orientation. During that time, it brings in an analyst from the training department to help it—the team's charter specified that it should use this resource. Then the team develops a plan to analyze salespersons' outputs, tasks, and knowledge and skill requirements and to conduct a gap analysis to see what knowledge and skills are lacking and how sales performance is being affected.

Based on these activities, the team designs a new training curriculum architecture to systematically inform, educate, and train the salespeople. Some courses are available commercially, whereas others have to be custom developed to fit the company's unique needs and product line specifics. An initial training program on win-win sales call planning and conduct is pilot-tested in one sales office, and it takes a few months to analyze the impact of sales results. If the pilot test is successful, the program is fully deployed in all other sales offices.

Overcoming Barriers

During Phase 2 design and test activities, your teams will probably encounter a number of obstacles. Here are some of the most common ones and ideas on ways to avoid or overcome them.

• *Excluding or ignoring key stakeholders.* Sometimes teams fail to include one or two key people who have the knowledge and skills to help a team carry out its design and test assignment effectively. Sometimes they fail to gather information from key sources, and they design and test without crucial data. For instance, a team may design a customer satisfaction measurement system without talking to customers—either the team believes it knows the customers well enough that it doesn't have to contact them or it's afraid to ask them questions that it assumes (wrongly) will offend them.

The solution here is to assess the specific information needs of each team at the start. That means questioning assumptions, such as "we know what our customers want," and examining all the stakeholders on the cube to see if they are or should be represented. It also means choosing team members from a process rather than a functional perspective—the process group should be more diverse and include more people with a multifunctional understanding than a purely functional group.

• *Getting stuck in the "team" process.* Many newly formed teams or teams without a great deal of project experience have trouble adapting to the new work methodology. They fall back on their functional roots and are too contentious to agree on a design and test project plan. Or, at the other extreme, they are so anxious to achieve consensus and avoid conflict that they rush forward before they've really hammered out all the issues—potentially valuable suggestions and challenges from each team member are missed by the artificial consensus, resulting in costly rework later on.

To overcome this barrier, use facilitators. Facilitators will keep things moving at the proper speed. They have excellent interpersonal skills; they can synthesize everyone's comments into a written statement (or set of statements) that everyone agrees to; they aren't afraid of the strong emotional conflicts that can be part of a successful group process. All these attributes enable facilitators to enhance team and project efficacy. Facilitators can be internal employees or external consultants. External facilitators tend to be well suited to executive-level teams, where there may be explosive political issues on the table that an internal facilitator might want to avoid or that the executive leadership team might avoid with a subordinate in the room.

If you use an employee-facilitator, make sure she isn't facilitating in her functional area (because she'll find it difficult to separate herself from the content and perform her process facilitator role objectively). Also, avoid placing a middle-level facilitator in an executive-level team—the former may feel intimidated, and the latter may assume an executive posture rather than being the team players that a project demands.

• *Becoming a silo team.* Just as functional departments can have a silo mentality, so can cross-functional teams. Sometimes team isolation means that one team doesn't know what the other teams are doing. Team A is working on an improvement that will affect Team B's improvement, yet no effort has been made to coordinate the two teams' improvement activities. It's quite possible that both teams will design and test improvements successfully, but that during deployment the two improvements will affect each other negatively.

Ironically, teams that work especially well together are in danger of inadvertently divorcing themselves from the rest of the organization. Team members become so close and dependent on one another that they close ranks and shut everyone else out. In other words, they've taken teamwork one step too far.

To overcome this barrier to Phase 2 success, anticipate and plan for these issues in Phase 1. In many instances, you'll be able to see where different teams will overlap, where the effectiveness of one improvement is dependent on another. Building a communication component (between teams) into the plan will minimize the problems of isolated teams. In addition, monitor teams for signs of an "us versus them" mentality and take steps to remind them that every team must function within the whole and not as a separate part.

• *Forgetting crucial steps, logic, and details.* Phase 2 must be carried out in a highly organized, detail-oriented fashion. A "project" mindset is important. Little things such as lack of time or proper resources can cause significant delays or quality problems. The best way to avoid these problems is to be realistic. Specifically, when you create a project plan, always question whether your goals and actions are feasible. Are your due dates reasonable? Have you allowed team members sufficient time to complete their tasks (considering their other, daily job responsibilities)? Are all required resources properly identified and allocated so that team members will receive them when they need them?

One helpful tip here is to map project plan tasks in great detail. Vague, generalized instructions allow crucial activities to slip through the cracks. Detail when something should be done, by whom, and how. When it becomes apparent during the project that the original plan is impractical, the project plan should be updated to reflect reality.

Measuring Your Success

The final step of Phase 2 is evaluating your pilot test programs. Though there are many ways and tools to measure success, the charter you've created is the best tool available. What was the team chartered to do? To reduce cycle time and costs? To develop a customer satisfaction measurement system? To improve sales results through training? Whatever it was, that is your most important measure. If the pilot fell short of the charter, then it shouldn't be deployed. It's possible that a team will have to redesign the improvement and run another pilot test to meet its charter. This may require new team members, and there may be costly delays and griping from above and below.

But it's worth all these headaches if you can prevent a mediocre pilot from being more fully deployed. You are much better off if you front-end load your project with additional redesign and pilot testing of an improvement that will eventually be deployed more smoothly and successfully throughout the organization.

Chapter 8

Deploying With Strategic Intent

You can't take deployment for granted. Though logic might dictate that a successful pilot will translate into a successful deployment, this is not always so. In fact, many improvement teams stumble in the transition from Phase 2 to Phase 3, failing to manage and support deployment strategy. That's a big mistake, both literally and figuratively. Deployment is where you invest a great deal of time, money, and other resources. It's where you receive your biggest payoff if it is successful, and your biggest loss if it isn't.

In this chapter, we'll take you through this third improvement phase, from predeployment to postdeployment, and the measurements of success.

Getting Ready

Being prepared to deploy is as important as the deployment process itself. Before anything else is done, determine which team will manage and support deployment. Sometimes it will be the Phase 2 team that designed and tested the improvement, but not always. In either case, teams must be rechartered for the new phase—new training is often necessary.

Ideally, people at the deployment sites will have been involved from the beginning. Having anticipated that this deployment phase would come, you made sure that the right people were involved as early as Phase 1. If you haven't involved them, you shouldn't be shocked to learn that you'll have to make a special planning and training effort to secure their involvement and enthusiastic participation before and during deployment.

As much as possible, you should anticipate and plan to resolve integration issues. Improvements may have a significant impact on numerous areas, including organizational structure, job design, processes, measurement systems, and reward and recognition. For each targeted deployment site, evaluate where the impacts are and what steps should be taken to ensure that all the pieces fall into place.

How to Deploy

Identifying deployment sites and collecting information concerning customization requirements from those sites are crucial initial steps. Customizing the improvement design created in the previous phase is frequently necessary. One size does not typically fit all. Whether the site is a manufacturing plant or a sales office, it probably will vary in one way or another from the pilot site(s). The project plan, therefore, must incorporate the specific design changes for each site. You should assess training needs and figure out how to monitor and support improvements at each site before the actual deployment takes place. Use the resource infrastructure diagram (Exhibit 6-5) to assist you in this endeavor.

We've found that establishing an implementation team at each site is an excellent idea, especially if the improvement is an especially complex or difficult one. Implementation teams, like any other team, need to be chartered, trained, and provided with support (including support from the team that designed the improvement).

The plan should also set up the steps and the schedule for deploying improvements at sites.

The logic of deployment, however, starts unraveling under the pressure to move quickly, the frustration when a pilot improvement doesn't segue easily to a site, and the coordination difficulties when numerous sites are involved. To keep the logic intact and Phase 3 moving along at a reasonable pace, the following roadmap directions will prove helpful.

• *Deploy to sites sequentially rather than simultaneously.* If you try to deploy an improvement everywhere at once, you run the risk of stretching your resources too thin. By doing it one site (or a few sites) at a time, you reduce this risk and give yourself the opportunity to learn something from each deployment site that you can use at the next one.

• *Look at each deployment site as a mini-pilot test.* This follows from the previous point. Just because you're deploying an improvement doesn't mean you're done designing (or redesigning) it. You'll probably have to do a number of fixes, and each fix may give you valuable information that will increase the efficacy of the improvement. From the data gleaned, you may find it's necessary to redesign the improvement at all sites—you want the improvement to be consistent throughout the organization.

• *Target areas of expected resistance.* Expect and anticipate resistance from certain deployment sites. Ideally, you'll have planned how to deal with this resistance in Phase 1. Here, you need to develop programs—training, incentives, and so on—that melt the resistance and facilitate buy-ins. It's also wise to pay attention to the reasons behind the resistance. They may be good reasons. You may find that people at deployment sites resist your improvement because it's flawed in some way. Having the improvement team at the site formally chartered by the site leadership can be an important tool for reducing resistance.

• *Prioritize deployment sites according to expected value.* If you don't have the resources to deploy at all sites in a given time frame, use a Pareto chart to prioritize sites. In your pilot, you learned how to estimate your ROI for the improvement. Compare that return against the cost of deployment for each potential site. You may find you can only afford to deploy at a select group of sites or that your larger sites give you the most value.

• *Balance the consequences in favor of successful deployment.* When you deploy an improvement, you're asking every team member to take actions that have consequences. Are the consequences positive or negative, and what are the long-term consequences versus the short-term ones? Let's say an improvement calls for salespeople to fill out sales call sheets. Most sales people would view the consequence of this action as a short-term negative—they hate additional paperwork. As a result, they'll grumble and generally do a poor job of filling out their sales sheets. Beware negative short-term consequences; they carry far more weight than long-term ones. You can balance these negative consequences with positive short-term ones: training on the overall rationale and value of this new paperwork burden, measurement of adoption, and incentives, for instance.

Examples of Deployment Differences

The difficulty of deployment varies according to many factors. Generally, it's easier to deploy at six similar sites in the same geographical area than at hundreds of diverse sites spread over two continents. It tends to be easier to deploy an improvement in the business drivers part of the cube than in a business process such as manufacturing.

The customer satisfaction measurement system discussed previously can be deployed with relative ease. Though it's important to monitor the progress of deployment and see if it hits a snag with certain types of customers, this deployment doesn't require a tremendous amount of logistical support.

Deploying a process at plants, as illustrated by the middle management example, is much more difficult. Setting up teams in each plant, obtaining baseline data, implementing and testing improvements, and evaluating those data to determine if cycle time and costs have been reduced all require people, hours, and resources.

Our third example, deploying a sales training program at various sales offices, requires a different set of deployment tools and actions. Because each sales office may have a different market and customers with special needs, the sales skills used successfully in the pilot may not work as well at other offices. If comparing the new data received from an office during deployment with the baseline data reveals that the improved sales training program isn't working, adjustments in the design may have to be made for a given office.

Let's look at another example of deployment, this time focusing on the infrastructure impact. You're in the process of deploying a new, computerized cash register system at all your stores throughout the country. In each store, there are a variety of customer/stakeholders, each with varying concerns. The clerks who have to use the new machines are worried about how these machines may slow them down and create long lines of upset customers; the store manager is concerned about the overtime to deliver training programs for the clerks to help them use the machines effectively; the regional manager is worried about the up-front costs, which will result in a temporarily unattractive profit-and-loss statement.

None of these worries may have surfaced in your pilot. Your team poured so much enthusiasm, time, and effort into the test that everyone in the pilot store was constantly reassured and ignored every negative in the pursuit of a successful pilot. During deployment, however, that constant reassurance is often lacking, and the result is a negative chain reaction. If you haven't provided sales clerks with sufficient training, they won't maximize the potential of the new technology. If you haven't made it clear that an initial, temporarily unattractive profit-and-loss statement won't be viewed as a black mark, regional managers won't support their store managers' training costs.

The solution, of course, is to address the issues that you've determined will crop up in each store. By addressing employees' worries with appropriate training and other forms of support, you help deployment progress more smoothly.

During deployment, organizations should consider the needs not only of different groups of employees, but of different groups of customers. The following typical scenario illustrates this point. A company decides it's going to deploy an improvement in its inventory control system. Instead of printing numbers on the outside of boxes, it begins using bar codes. At first, everything proceeds smoothly; the new system enables the company to ship its older products before its newest products. Many of the company's large customers adjust well to the bar codes. But many of the small ones are lost—they've checked shipments by the numbers on the outside of the box for years, and they don't understand or like or have the equipment required for bar code technology. In a number of cases, these smaller customers look for other suppliers.

To avoid this scenario, rely on the roadmap's list of stakeholders. Not only during deployment but in all the phases, consider the impact of an improvement on each stakeholder.

Overcoming Barriers

Although there are scores of potential obstacles to successful deployment, a few recur with numbing regularity. Be on the lookout for the following.

• *Insular deployment planning.* Organizations that fail to include key people from deployment sites in planning sessions run two major risks. First, they will lack the input necessary to predict if and what customization will be required. Second, they may be unable to gain managers' enthusiastic support for and participation in the deployment, resulting in grudging acceptance of the improvement at best and sabotage at worst.

• *Downplaying or ignoring "small" problems that manifest themselves during the pilot.* Minor glitches that arise in pilots often explode into crises during deployment. For instance, during the design and test phase, a process improvement eliminated the jobs of three people. They were transferred to other jobs, but when you deploy this same improvement to 100 locations, these three people become 300. The same situation frequently occurs with training. During the pilot, the team can give personal attention to each participant, holding his or her hand every step of the way. This type of personal attention may be impossible during full deployment, so that a completely different approach to the training is required. Deployment is often a massive undertaking. Never assume that little problems encountered during tests will disappear later on—they may in fact grow.

• *Rigged tests.* Perhaps they're not rigged intentionally, but the result is the same: What worked so well in the pilot fails on a larger scale. Part of the problem is that people are often hand-picked to participate in pilot programs—not only are they the best people, but they're given abundant resources, such as consultants and trainers, and the spotlight of attention is focused on their work. It's often difficult to replicate the resources or the attention level at deployment locations, and as a result, deployment fails to deliver the process improvements reported in the pilot.

The alternative is to carefully assess what skills and resources are critical—the ones that made the pilot work and that are feasible for deployment. If you assume that every group in your organization has the same skills as those in the test, you will have made a false assumption.

Some pilot tests are successful only because everyone was in the spotlight. Like a sports team that performs over its head in the big game, many pilot participants give extra effort to make the pilot fly. They work harder than they've ever worked before; they break rules to keep the improvement on track; they neglect other responsibilities and spend a lot of money to avoid failure. As a result, the improvement was successful in test. But you can't and don't want to duplicate these things in deployment. Heroic efforts are admirable, but you can't deploy heroics continuously.

• *Speeding.* Let's say your process improvement was spectacularly successful in the pilot. Your executive-level team is so excited about the results that it can't wait to deploy—it rolls out the improvement fast and furiously.

We know of an automotive company that was deploying process improvements in its plants. One plant, where the UAW presence was especially strong, eventually rebelled. It wasn't that the union objected to the improvements themselves; the cross-training, robotics, and other measures all received union approval. What it didn't approve of were the accompanying layoffs that came without warning. The union rank-and-file was outraged and threw out the union leadership that initially acquiesced to the improvements. From that point on, the union was dead set against any program that contained the words "improvement" or "quality." The stakeholder requirements and effects had not been fully assessed.

The point here is to slow down, analyze, and plan before moving from Phase 2 to Phase 3. You can't anticipate deployment problems if you don't give yourself adequate time to do so.

• *Saying one thing, doing another.* A number of years ago, we announced to our staff that we didn't care about when they came to work or when they went home, as long as they met objectives. The first time someone strolled in at 11:00, however, we had to bite our tongues.

Be prepared for employees to test you, to see if the company is really going to walk the talk. Let's say a team comes to you and says it requires more resources to facilitate implementation of improvements. But the team adds that allocating those additional resources will result in a temporary, but sizable loss for the quarter. Do you say, "Full steam ahead with deployment and damn the cost," or do you shut down and fret over the books? If it's the latter, you may appear fickle about your commitment to deploying improvements.

The following analogy may help you stick to the course. Let's say you've played tennis for years, but then decide to take lessons. When you try to incorporate the lesson specifics into your game, your performance suffers initially: It feels awkward to grip the racquet the way the instructor taught you, you seem to have lost the ball control you once had, and you may be tempted to resume your old habits. But if you persist in trying to make the new method work, your performance will eventually improve and then become self-reinforcing.

Prepare yourself and your people for a possible temporary decline in performance during the early deployment phase. As long as the temporary decline is anticipated and no one panics when it occurs, you'll overcome this barrier.

Measures of Success

Just because you say it's deployed doesn't mean this is so. We've seen many examples of organizations that issue orders for improvements to be deployed and automatically assume that these orders are being carried out. In fact, they may not have been carried out or they may have been implemented haphazardly.

Measures should be established before you deploy. Not measure, but measures. Partial measures won't suffice. Typically, the following three measures are called for:

- Deployment progress (number of sites successfully completed compared to planned timeline)
- Performance gain (ways in which improvement has met strategic objectives)
- Costs

Without these measures, accountability will be absent. Every employee should understand not only that he or she will be held accountable, but what he or she will be held accountable for.

Deployment should never be something you just "do." It doesn't take place in a vacuum. Every division and every employee has responsibilities—the daily work of producing products and services can't stop just to implement improvements. Because you have only so much time, money, and energy to spare, and because you have to keep the business running, deployment must be approached strategically. You're not going to be able to deploy every improvement at every site simultaneously. You have to choose where you'll deploy and when strategically, from the standpoint of what will help the business most. Establishing measures will enable you to determine if you've hit the strategic mark with your deployment.

Chapter 9
Integration

At the risk of sounding like nags, we've emphasized the need to address integration issues in each of Chapters 6 through 8. We've insisted that it's never too early to work on integration, that it should start in Phase 1 and continue through each following phase. Even though integration is the fourth phase numerically, it's not something that can be left for last.

Our definition of integration relates to all the phases: finding and fixing disconnects between new, improved processes and infrastructure elements or between infrastructure elements and other linkages. Disconnects are unavoidable: Improving a process means changing a process, and when you change one thing, you may have to change another or they won't "fit." At the same time, however, disconnects are all too easy to overlook. More than one organization has basked in the glow of its magnificent improvements, only to reach Phase 4 and realize to its chagrin that "the rewards and recognition system is sending the wrong message." It's sending the wrong message because no one changed it so that it was integrated with the wonderful new and improved processes. Everyone was so focused on making key improvements work that necessary infrastructure resources were allowed to disconnect.

Disconnects can be identified and fixed in any phase. In Phase 1, disconnects can be anticipated while improvements are being planned. In Phase 2, they can be spotted in the pilot. In Phase 3, they surface during deployment. Before, during, and at the end of each phase, opportunities exist to correct the integration problem.

Ideally, Phase 4 will be a clean-up of the disconnects that somehow slipped through the cracks. Since some of those disconnects can be very important to the success of improvements, this should never be minimized. But a clean-up operation is infinitely preferable and infinitely easier than confronting massive disconnects that have been ignored until after deployment.

Assessing and Identifying the Disconnects

After you've deployed improvements in Phase 3, you can look at those improvements within the context of the front face of the roadmap cube. Because you've carefully mapped out the connections among all the processes and metrics, business drivers, and infrastructure resources, you've established the multiple linkages of your business. Therefore, you can now look at the pertinent section of the map and assess the disconnects caused by a deployed improvement.

When doing so, you should keep the team that designed the deployment intact. It, along with the teams that implemented improvements at various sites, has a bird's-eye view of where the disconnects are. The next step is a formal analysis of integration issues. By formal, we mean systematically looking at all the linkages and assessing them for disconnects or dysfunctionality. This assessment should lead to one or a family of project plans to clean up the important integration issues.

To Do It or Not to Do It

This analysis may require your teams to analyze the importance of each disconnect relative to performance. Some disconnects may not have much impact on performance and can be ignored (for now). A Pareto analysis of the cost and benefits of fixing disconnects and recommendations to the executive leadership team of which ones to fix usually is helpful. Typically, some disconnects are fixed in Phase 4, whereas others may be able to wait until later.

Disconnects are not always easy to spot. Some are obscured or hidden by seemingly larger, more immediate issues. To help you identify them, the following checklist of disconnect symptoms should be helpful.

- People in one department, division, or plant are complaining that another group is violating corporate policies and procedures.
- A business process improvement has proved incompatible with at least one support process.
- External stakeholders tell you that your "new way" of doing things isn't as good as your old way.
- You see "work-around" systems springing up to circumvent problems caused by improvements.
- Various work groups refuse to embrace an improvement because of fears about rising costs.

- Your reward systems cause employees to reject or sabotage new systems and methods rather than accept them.
- You're encountering a great deal of resistance to deployed changes from vice-presidents in different groups and divisions.

Different Types of Integration Problems

To give you a sense of the types of integration scenarios you might encounter, let's look at the executive-, middle management–, and working-level examples used in Chapter 7.

On the executive level, you've deployed a new customer satisfaction measurement system. You may have missed the disconnects between that new system and the old rewards and recognition system. For instance, executives receive bonuses based on criteria that have nothing to do with satisfying customers. It's conceivable that you could have designed, tested, and deployed a customer satisfaction system that was excellent in every way save one: Bonuses weren't linked to customer satisfaction.

A middle management team was charged with optimizing operations across production scheduling, manufacturing, and distribution. Again, the process was greatly improved, and there was no hint that something was wrong until people working with the new process began to complain that the MIS system was not providing timely, appropriate data for effective daily decision making. Because the MIS system had not been improved to support decision making within the new process, a disconnect occurred.

On the working level, a sales order entry process improvement is deployed. The disconnect takes place in policies and procedures. That disconnect can be caused by any one of a number of oversights, including:

- People are still using the forms and other materials from the old process.
- There has been inadequate training to maximize the benefits of the new process.
- People currently in the system have been trained in the improved process, but entry-level training hasn't been brought up to speed, so new people are being trained the old way.
- Policy and procedures manuals have not been rewritten to conform with the improved process.

You should also be aware of a very common and potentially devastating (if ignored) integration scenario that may affect all levels. When you change (improve) a process, you change the very nature of the jobs related to that process. If you don't recognize the "cascading" effect of the changed process on jobs, you may be inviting disconnects. It's possible that a process change can affect a job's training requirements, selection criteria, and performance appraisal. You may find that with an improved process, people are being selected, trained, and appraised for a job that no longer exists. Any major process change requires revisiting the design of the organization structure, jobs, and work teams.

Barriers

As much as you may want to integrate your improvements, you may find that a number of barriers stand in your way. These barriers often have been part of the company culture for years; they frequently are ingrained in the infrastructure. To clear them from your path, you first have to recognize them as threats to improvements rather than benign traditions and practices.

1. *Performance appraisal systems that discourage team effort.* These systems may demand that managers give a numerical rank to their employees. The problem, of course, is that even if all your employees are doing a good job, someone still must be ranked at the top and the bottom. Your top-ranked and bottom-ranked people will resist working together, and that destroys the conceptual framework for a team. During deployment, performance appraisal may not have been a big issue as everyone focused on the technical aspects of installing an improvement. But after the dust settles and the routine returns, the performance appraisal system can catalyze disconnects. It can create cognitive dissonance between what management preaches and what it practices, resulting in people whose goals are a personal high ranking rather than the team's continuous improvement.

2. *Punishing managers for not using their entire budget.* Continuous improvement efforts require financial flexibility: If one department doesn't use all its budget, another department that needs funds should receive them. But in many organizations, if managers don't use their entire budget, they receive a smaller budget the following year. The system should be changed so that it encourages staying under budget. This way, dollars can be fairly distributed among departments or teams

and won't remain locked up in separate treasure chests. Disconnects between teams can occur because of a perceived inequity in resource allocation. Resentment can build when Team A receives far more than it needs and Team B receives far less simply because Team A knows how to play the budget-request game.

3. *Maintaining the traditional management job evaluation system.* One of the toughest integration issues involves streamlining staff, combining job functions, and eliminating unnecessary positions. It's a tough issue because the job evaluation system typically rewards empire building. Job rank and corresponding pay are traditionally dependent on how many dollars and people a given job controls. Everyone has an incentive to pad the payroll rather than reduce it, since size counts. Since many improvements depend on streamlining staff to some extent, the job evaluation system must be revamped to reflect that goal. Disconnects occur here because managers place quantity over quality. Many job evaluation systems have no provision for team structures or for individual contributor career ladders, both of which are major features of the new organizational landscape.

4. *Sustaining a culture in which honesty and open communication take a backseat to finger pointing.* One of the secrets of integration is a culture that tolerates mistakes, that does not manipulate or deceive the rank and file, that encourages everyone to share concerns and ideas without fear of recrimination in order to fix problems, not blame. Without this type of open culture, integration is a nightmare.

After successfully deploying a number of improvements, an organization learns that everything isn't going as smoothly as it had hoped. One division is requesting an unexpectedly large appropriation to make adjustments to systems; managers are feuding over ways to keep new and improved processes moving forward; a team was caught reporting misleading results, making deployment appear more successful than it really was.

To avoid or resolve these problems isn't as easy as it might seem. Many times, management faces a dilemma in the integration phase, as the following story illustrates.

A brand manager for a Fortune 500 company requests $1 million in additional funds to help make adjustments in the marketing of the product line, adjustments necessitated by the continuous improvement program that was recently deployed. The brand manager has done his homework—he's outlined an attractive return-on-investment scenario to his superiors.

But top management turns the request down without exception. Of course, this blunt veto creates estrangement among all the employees who work on the product line. Management has been preaching openness and honesty for months, yet the unexplained veto seems to be a contradiction.

What employees didn't realize was that management had decided to drop the product line at the end of the year and introduce a new one, a decision dictated by results from the deployment. It didn't want to tell employees that this was the reason for the veto because it was afraid the competition would get wind of its new product introduction plans.

To deal with these dilemmas—which are becoming increasingly common—management has to learn to use its communication capabilities creatively. In this instance, it might have sat down months before with all the brand managers and said something like: "Look, when the deployment is completed and you start trying to get everything back on track, some of you may come to us with requests for additional funds. And in some instances, we're going to have to turn you down and not give you a reason why. We don't want to do this, but we're worried about leaks, which we've had in the past. So we're going to ask you to bear with us for a little while until we can explain the reason for our actions."

5. *Allowing measurement systems to become or to be perceived as punitive in nature.* Every improvement requires various measures—it's essential that you determine degrees of improvement. Yet in the past, measurement systems were punitive tools. They were like hidden monitors, watching employees and spotting them when they made a mistake. For years, these measures were trotted out by management to chastise employees or groups for errors.

It's time to change employee perception of measurement systems. You should foster an appreciation of what these systems can teach employees. If you don't convince employees that measures are a positive rather than a negative tool, they'll hide data from management or distort the data, fearing that the information will be used against them. When data suggest a problem, bring employees together in a problem-solving team to deal with it rather than allowing it to become a nasty little secret.

Disconnects are sustained by fear. Rather than confronting problems or difficult situations caused by improvements, people avoid them because they're worried about "looking bad." Perhaps the true test of management's willingness to stick to its improvement path comes in Phase 4: The organization discovers unexpected disconnects caused by improvements, and business suffers as a result. If management starts blaming people for the disconnects and resulting revenue falloff, it will ensure that no one will ever take a risk on an improvement again. It's sending a message that short-term bad news is not okay, even if it's a result of a long-term improvement strategy. It's far better to simply fix the problem rather than fixing the blame.

Integration Facilitation

Most of the problems discussed in this chapter can be avoided. With a keen awareness of integration issues in all the roadmap phases, you can bring disparate parts together. Here are a few do's and don'ts:

• *Do tackle integration issues before the last minute or the final phase.* We can't overemphasize this point. Even though integration is the fourth phase, it should be planned for and dealt with in the earlier three phases. Sometimes you can anticipate obvious integration difficulties. Other times, you can identify integration issues and test integration solutions in Phase 2. The worst thing to do is to let all the integration issues pile up and find yourself overwhelmed in Phase 4. There aren't many worse feelings than to have deployed your improvements, think you're well on your way to winning the Baldrige Award, and then realize that your MIS system no longer delivers the right information to the right people at the right time. Prioritize integration issues, and deal with crucial ones early and often.

• *Don't sacrifice long-term goals for short-term gains.* Integration is where your long-term resolve is tested. A training company, through customer satisfaction research, learns that its customers prefer all their training materials to have the same "look." The training company, however, has just spent hundreds of thousands of dollars on new brochures and other materials that are tailored to different levels—the materials for supervisors look radically different from those for line workers. The short-term option: Use the brochures for as long as the inventory lasts and Band-Aid hurt customer relationships. The long-term option: Eat the cost of dumping the training materials and start over from scratch, confident that such a move will cement customer relationships, sharing research results with customers as an interim step.

• *Do search for your integration problems.* We've seen many companies make it through the deployment phase, then sit back and admire the scenery. They've successfully implemented some key improvements, and they're happy. So what if everything isn't meshing smoothly, they rationalize, we reduced cycle time, and that's enough. But when the spotlight fades from improvements, that's when the disconnects begin to do their damage. When the spotlight was on, everyone was performing at peak levels, doing their best to hold the improvements together. But when things return to "normal," the lack of an improvement-congruent reward and recognition system (or some other type of disconnect) will become an issue—employees will realize that they're rewarded for behavior that has nothing to do with continuous improvement goals. Your improvement may look as if it's solid and rolling along, but one good jolt on a bad road will cause the jury-rigged pieces to disconnect.

So when are you done? When is your integration work finished? Never. You should constantly monitor improvements for signs of disconnects. The litmus test is when all the implementations are done and a new routine has been established. If no major disconnects appear at this point, you've probably done an excellent job with integration, and Phase 4 will be the relatively easy clean-up effort it's supposed to be.

Chapter 10

Roles of the Road: Working Within a Team Structure

As you read about the roadmap in Chapter 9, you may have thought to yourself, "To use this roadmap, our top management must become totally (not partially) involved with all aspects of the improvement process." That's a shock to many people. The assumption has always been that involvement is necessary only at the working level—from the people who actually implement the improvements. Typically, top management confines its efforts to dictating and motivating: "Do actions A, B, and C, and I know you can do it because you're the best-trained and smartest people we have."

That's no longer sufficient. Nor is it sufficient for management to get together during a brief staff meeting, divvy up responsibilities, assign tasks to subordinates, and go on to "more important" operational matters like figuring out how to produce more widgets daily or placate a particularly demanding customer. Total Quality Management demands not only top management's complete and continuous involvement, but the same sustained participation from all levels, including middle management.

The question, of course, is how to secure that type of involvement at all levels. The answer is in this chapter and Chapter 11. We've created a team structure and identified key roles within that structure that will facilitate everyone's involvement in your quality effort. It's a strong hierarchical structure that will enable you to deploy strategy, policy, and empowerment downward through a chain of sponsorship, and that will feed results back up through that chain. It's also the ideal structure and roles for using the roadmap.

Exhibit 10-1 should give you a sense of how such a structure might look.

Executive Leadership Team

At the top of the hierarchy is the executive leadership team. Composed of top management, this team has a number of crucial roles, including:

- Establishing mission, vision, and values
- Developing business architecture using the front face of the roadmap cube
- Establishing executive-level owners of key processes
- Conducting company-level assessments
- Developing company-level improvement plans and priorities
- Establishing, sponsoring, and chartering process steering teams
- Establishing, sponsoring, and chartering company-level improvement project teams
- Mapping company-level leadership processes
- Ensuring integration of improvement projects
- Managing empowerment and accountability of subordinate teams
- Advocating and communicating TQM concepts, goals, and structure inside and outside the business

Let's look at some of these roles in a bit more detail. When this team assesses, plans, and prioritizes improvement opportunities, it will find this role greatly facilitated by the front face of the roadmap cube. Instead of working on these important tasks in a random fashion, the team will find that the front face provides a framework. It offers the team direction as to what processes it should map (as opposed to what others should do). For instance, the team is responsible for detailed mapping of leadership processes such as strategic planning and the overall TQM effort. On the other hand, mapping the sales process can be delegated to the sales process steering team (steering teams are responsible for specific processes, locations, facilities, or subordinate business units).

The executive-level team must establish these steering teams, determining who should be on a given team and what teams should be set up first. Most organizations find that it makes sense to set up three or four steering teams corresponding to three to six high-priority improvement opportunities; other lower-priority improvements and teams get

Exhibit 10-1. TQM team structure.

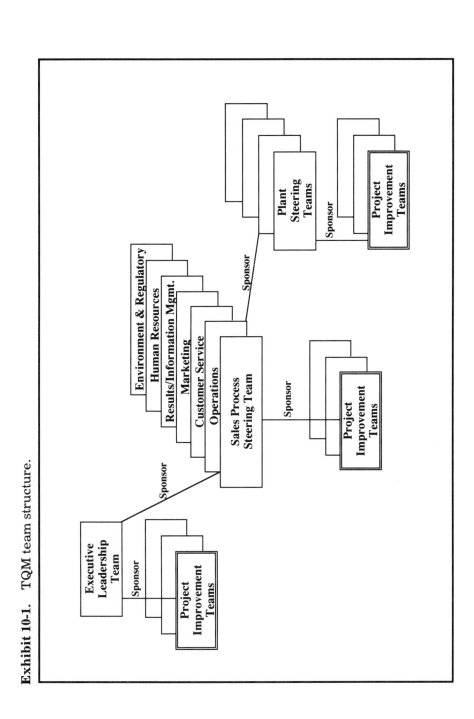

set up months or even years later. The executive-level team also is responsible for chartering these steering teams.

Sponsorship of teams is another critical responsibility that is frequently neglected; we'll discuss the roles of sponsors later in this chapter.

Integration is another executive-level responsibility. As you improve a process, you're changing it, and a changed process probably won't fit (or integrate) with other aspects of the company, such as the MIS system, the rewards and recognition system, and other processes. The executive team must use the front face of the roadmap to monitor the linkages among all these elements, anticipating and planning for disconnects caused by improvements or fixing the disconnects when they occur. It can do so in scores of ways: placing a common member on the sales and manufacturing process steering teams in order to encourage integration, for instance.

Finally, the executive-level team must actively and constantly promote the company's improvement efforts to all customer-stakeholders. This may mean the CEO talking about TQM to his or her employees in meetings, memos, and even one-on-one sessions. It should involve top management communicating how improvements will help meet key business goals. It also means sending the TQM message to people outside the organization. Everyone from community leaders to the government to suppliers should realize that top managers have become fervent disciples and practitioners of TQM.

This shouldn't be all talk and no action; top managers have to shift their focus and time from operational matters to systemic change. The role of TQM leader is one that the CEO can never shirk. In a major corporation with multiple business units, divisions, or subsidiaries that act like independent or semi-independent businesses, you will need an executive leadership team for each.

Steering Teams

These teams can be process or leadership teams for a major location or organization unit such as a plant or sales region. Their roles include:

- Identifying function/process business architecture
- Conducting assessments
- Devising improvement plan and priorities (based on company plan)
- Building a function/process-level measurement hierarchy

- Establishing, sponsoring, and chartering improvement team projects
- Mapping and improving selected processes
- Ensuring integration
- Managing empowerment and accountability of improvement teams
- Providing support and resources to improvement teams
- Reporting results to the executive leadership team

These tasks are similar in many ways to those of the executive leadership team. Again, a steering team maps processes using the front face of the roadmap cube. But rather than mapping all processes, it focuses on its particular process (or plant) and how that process is linked to other processes. Within its designated process, the team searches for improvement opportunities, prioritizes them, and determines how each fits into the overall business strategy handed down by the executive-level team.

The steering team deploys strategy down to the next level in the form of improvement project teams. Just as the executive-level team did with it, each steering team will sponsor and charter improvement project teams, providing resources and other types of support.

Improvement Project Teams

The roles for these teams include:

- Preparing project plans
- Assessing improvement potential
- Designing and testing improvements
- Preparing deployment plans
- Overseeing and supporting deployment
- Reporting deployment results
- Assessing integration issues
- Recommending or negotiating integration with other processes and systems

If you'll pardon a cliché that fits with our map metaphor, this is where the rubber meets the road. Or, to put it another way, this is where improvements get made. The role of these teams begins with a project plan that should be achievable within given time and resource parameters. The four-phase side of the roadmap cube provides the "how to do it" for a team. The last three phases, especially, should guide its project planning efforts.

We should emphasize that these teams can operate on any level. One team may be composed of executive leadership team members and be working on high-level projects; another team may be on the middle management level; a third may be at the plant (or working) level looking at a machining improvement. There can and should be cross-linkage of team membership. For instance, someone may be a member of both the executive leadership team and a project improvement team.

Sponsors

We've mentioned sponsors a few times in this chapter, and if you turn back to Exhibit 10-1, you'll find sponsors forming the connecting lines between different types of teams. Sponsors play crucial if unfamiliar (to people unfamiliar with TQM) roles in the team structure. Those roles include:

- Chartering a steering or improvement project team relative to its:
  —Purpose
  —Membership
  —Expected deliverables
  —Limits of empowerment
  —Reporting requirements
- Acting as an advocate for the team
- Helping the team obtain resources and information
- Helping the team clear organizational roadblocks and integrate with other efforts
- Providing reward and recognition to the team and team members

Given these diverse and potentially challenging tasks, sponsors must be carefully chosen. They should have a major stake in what their teams accomplish (a manufacturing vice-president is a logical choice as the sponsor of a manufacturing process steering team, for instance), and they should be able to handle political issues that may come up, cutting through red tape and securing resources needed by their teams.

Ideally, every member of the executive-level team will have an opportunity to be a sponsor. It exposes them to a new form of management, one in which they serve the team rather than having subordinates serve them.

Sponsorship is a proactive rather than a reactive role. Instead of sitting back and waiting for requests for resources, the sponsor should anticipate team needs. Though the sponsor may not attend every team meeting, he or she has to be involved in more than a distant, superficial way. One aspect of that involvement is management of team accountability: The sponsor contracts with the team to finish a project by a certain time within established resources limits; if this can't be done, the team has to renegotiate its charter with the sponsor.

The sponsor may also be the process owner—the sponsor of the human resources process steering team may also be the human resources vice-president, for example. In other instances, however, the sponsor and the process owner are different people—for example, a line vice-president may sponsor a team charged with reengineering the company's training process and systems.

Ultimately, sponsors link every team in the organization back to the executive leadership team. They ensure that no team will dangle or be operating without a clout-wielding "lobbyist" for its particular improvement project. Without sponsors, it would be difficult if not impossible for this team structure to function effectively. With them, the downward flow of strategy, deployment, empowerment, and accountability is greatly enhanced, and integration can be managed.

CEO/General Manager

Here are the essential roles for the chief executive/general managers within this team structure:

- Chairing the executive leadership team
- Providing TQM strategic direction
- Providing resources
- Providing rewards and consequences
- Holding teams and executives accountable for results
- Issuing TQM implementation edicts

These roles mandate that the CEO be more than the "royalty" of the organization's quality initiative, delegating improvement responsibilities to others. He or she must be an active leader, and these roles suggest tasks that will keep the chief executive intimately involved in all phases of the improvement process. The mandate for change and the staying power to see it through must come from the top. The top officer must demonstrate a strong personal commitment through actions and words or the other officers will not take the effort seriously and the entire TQM approach will be weakened.

Wrong Roles, False Assumptions

Assigning the wrong roles to the right people happens frequently. The following are four common false assumptions that lead to mismatched role assignments.

False Assumptions

1. *One person has complete power and absolute responsibility for making quality work.* We've seen this scenario in countless corporations. An organization assigns all power and authority to its designated quality executive, giving her or him a mandate to implement TQM across the entire business. This expert may receive the CEO's stamp of approval, have access to many resources, and be given a reasonable time frame. The problem: The quality expert and his or her staff are separated from the mainstream business. Their focus is on TQM implementation, a long-term issue; the functional and process owners are focused on getting products and services delivered, a short-term issue. Any quality initiative is doomed to fail under these circumstances.

One of our clients was in this position. We were meeting with the company's beleaguered quality champion, who was futilely trying to get his isolated quality group to accomplish certain goals. When we explained to him the need to define and assign other roles in the organization within the context of quality objectives, he looked up at us, amazed and delighted, saying, "Thank God; I thought I was going to have to do all this myself!"

The lesson: If you assign all responsibility to one person or one group, you will be unsuccessful. You must assign the various roles discussed in this chapter to appropriate people throughout your organization.

2. *Top management's TQM role is relatively minor.* With all the talk of participative management and delegating decision-making power to lower levels, top managers frequently assume that there's not much for them to do when it comes to quality. After the big initial push in which the CEO and other top managers stress their commitment to TQM in memos and speeches, they seem to distance themselves, focusing instead on running the business. They fall back on old models, methods, and behaviors.

Such a low profile will eventually destroy employees' enthusiasm for and belief in TQM. If top management isn't taking an active, visible role in the effort, why should anyone else? If they're not changing their behaviors, why should anyone else? The most damaging effect of top management inactivity, though, is the lack of top-down strategic focus on targets of opportunity. Such a focus will not only dramatically improve business performance but will provide the mechanism to integrate improvements across the business.

One of the critical behaviors of a CEO, and one of the least appreciated, is to issue an edict to implement TQM. On the surface, an edict may seem to contradict the participative management philosophy associated with TQM. But participative management is the "how" that follows the "what" of the edict that champions TQM. The edict clearly communicates that there's no freedom of choice: Either you participate in TQM or you're out. Employees have to understand that management is serious about TQM and making it work.

3. *Failing to define roles and responsibilities of subordinates clearly, especially in relation to their empowerment.* Empowerment isn't a no-strings-attached deal. No one should be allowed complete freedom to make major decisions, especially if he or she hasn't earned that right. Yet empowerment is frequently misunderstood. That's why we see TQM efforts where managers at all levels are reluctant to empower anyone, or, even worse, where they empower in word and disempower in deed.

Parameters need to be set on the decision-making responsibilities of employees and managers up and down the line. Empowerment isn't automatic; it's earned in stages. Communicating a policy that decision-making authority expands with time and experience will temper expectations regarding empowerment for everyone involved in the organization's TQM efforts.

4. *Any improvement activity is acceptable, as long as there's activity.* Some quality gurus preach that anyone who wants to set up a quality improvement effort should do so. Their rationale is that it doesn't matter what quality improvement opportunity people start on (even if it's a water cooler issue) as long as they start on something, that once they gain experience using quality-based tools and techniques, they'll go on to bigger and better things. We've found that people often don't go on to anything bigger and better. Instead, teams start focusing their improvement efforts on narrow issues—they focus on optimizing things that benefit them directly, like saving themselves from doing jobs they dislike or concentrating on "fun" projects that don't achieve larger

corporate goals. This localized optimization may, in fact, cost a lot without returning any real benefits to the company.

We believe in targeted quality management in the initial implementation efforts. Selected with care and precision, improvements will yield meaningful business results that in turn will foster the enthusiasm and support necessary to sustain continuous improvements in the coming years.

A Vital, Never-Ending Role

Executive leadership can't abdicate its TQM role. That may seem like an obvious point—and one we've made before—but it's so important that it's worth belaboring the obvious. Too often, top managers get distracted from the quality effort by seemingly more pressing business concerns, or they fall back on old behaviors and delegate TQM responsibilities, removing themselves from the fray.

But without executive leadership involvement, you will fail in pursuing strategic targets of improvement, in deployment of improvements across the business, and in integration of improvements. You'll find yourself with numerous improvement teams, each going its own way, separate and unequal.

Committed and involved executive leadership can prevent this from happening and keep teams connected and moving toward key business goals.

Leading and overseeing the work of change, renewal, and reengineering of the business *is* the new work of top management.

Chapter 11

TQM Support Structure

The TQM team structure won't stand on its own, at least not for very long. It needs to be supported. The problem isn't a flaw in the team structure but the nature of TQM. This is a very complex endeavor, and without a support system, teams will find themselves lacking what they need to achieve improvement goals—there are so many pieces to the puzzle, it's easy to lose or overlook some of them. Organizations learn too late that a data storage system should have been in place so that teams could draw upon all the "paper" maps and reports created by other teams. Or management finally comes to realize that teams aren't making much progress because they lack a facilitator who understands team dynamics.

By the time organizations realize they need a support structure, it's often too late. Improvements have stalled, top management is disgruntled, budgets have been cut, and inertia has set in. The TQM support structure should be in place from the beginning.

A support structure can't consist of only one person. Yet that's exactly what happens in many organizations. As we mentioned earlier, one individual is designated Quality Champion or some similar title and expected to handle the massive requirements of any TQM effort. While a Quality Champion may provide some support, he or she cannot offer the systematic, companywide assistance that is necessary. For that, organizations require a support infrastructure.

Mapping the TQM Processes

We've broken down the TQM process into three subprocesses: leadership, product and service, and support (see Exhibit 11-1). In this chapter, we're going to focus on support and its four components.

Exhibit 11-1. TQM processes.

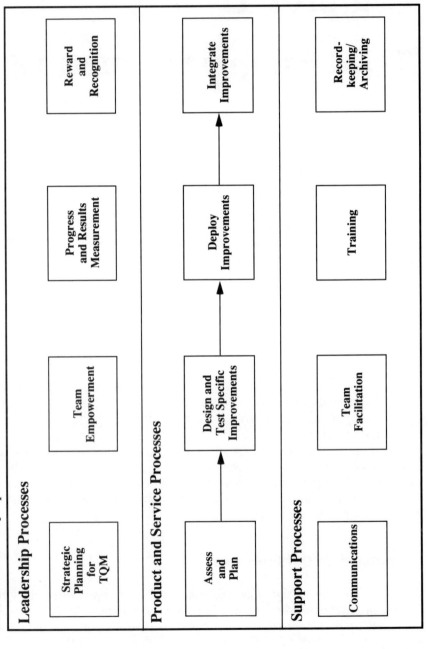

1. *Communication.* Information is at the heart of TQM. It provides teams with data crucial to their improvements; it lifts morale; it can be part of the organization's reward system (an improvement team being featured in the company newsletter, for instance). The key here is to determine what existing communication systems can be used to support TQM and to create new ones if necessary. To do so, answer key questions, such as:

- Who are your major customer/stakeholder groups, and what information do they need to support TQM?
- What are the best information channels to get them what they need?
- Are those channels in place, and can you capitalize on existing internal communication systems?

2. *Team facilitation.* Most organizations are aware of the value of facilitators in TQM. But they're unaware that most people make poor facilitators. The assumption that if you're a good trainer, you're a good facilitator is false. Facilitating is very different from training, and often more demanding. Facilitators require multiple skills above and beyond imparting information, and no one can learn these skills in a two-day seminar on facilitating. We'll talk about the facilitator's role later in this chapter.

3. *Training.* Training doesn't cold store. One of the biggest TQM training mistakes is to teach people something that they won't use for months or even years, especially technical tools such as statistical process control. We've found that many organizations overspend on training, teaching their people as much as they can as quickly as they can about TQM. It's much more cost-effective to target your training as you target your improvements, giving teams what they need when they need it.

A good analogy is the military's logistics function. It makes sure the food, transportation, and other supplies are there to support the fighting forces. Ideally, when a team is ready to embark on an improvement, the support will be there so that the team won't have to worry about anything but that improvement.

We've found that it's useful to brief teams at the beginning about various improvement tools: When they might use them, how, and why, and the training available to learn the tools. Then, when the time comes that it needs a tool, the team knows enough to request it.

4. *Recordkeeping/archiving.* It's not that teams don't grasp the importance of keeping a record of their work, it's that there are so many records of so much work that a lot of it becomes lost for lack of a systematic approach. As teams go through the improvement process, they generate project plans, milestone reports, process maps. All these are valuable to the TQM process, and all are easily lost. Sometimes they're lost because a team is disbanded; when a new team is formed a year later, someone asks, "Wasn't there a team a year ago that worked on this project?" There was, but no one has a record of what it did. Sometimes reports disappear into the drawers of team leaders; sometimes they leave with people who are caught in downsizing. Ideally, organizations will create databases and archives that are accessible to everyone. Duplication of effort is avoided when teams learn that what they need has been done by another team, and time is saved when teams don't have to search for days or weeks for a specific report or map. Access to information from other areas can also vastly simplify integration.

The Roles

Three roles are essential if the support process is to provide teams with communication, facilitation, training, and recordkeeping:

- TQM director
- TQM support staff
- Facilitators

Let's examine each role and the related responsibilities. We think you'll be surprised at how much each role contributes to helping teams capitalize on all the tools and techniques of the quality movement, and how each role makes every team's assignment that much easier to complete.

Responsibilities of TQM Director (or Vice-President)

- Driving strategic planning for the TQM process
- Championing the TQM effort/system
- Facilitating the executive leadership team
- Building an external benchmarking network and involvement with quality associations
- Serving as linkage to awards and certifications (Baldrige, ISO 9000, etc.)

- Troubleshooting the TQM effort/system
- Interpreting results
- Managing the TQM support system

The TQM director is the keeper of the cube—at least the front face of the roadmap cube. He or she is the organization's expert in all matters relating to quality, the one who articulates the business architecture of the organization using the front face. Conceptually and operationally, the director understands how TQM is working in the organization: He or she is the owner of the TQM process.

The director's responsibilities are wide and varied. Internally, the director meets with the executive leadership team's chairperson (the CEO) and helps set the team's meeting agendas, document the results of the meetings, and make sure they're distributed to appropriate teams. The support here allows the CEO to focus on pure leadership tasks rather than activities that take away from his or her main role. Externally, the TQM director establishes a network with best-in-class companies, helps the organization go after the Baldrige Award or ISO 9000 certification, and joins quality associations such as CCI.

Troubleshooting is the director's job. Every organization, even if it follows our roadmap instructions with care, will experience some problems along the way. A sponsor may fail to get a team adequate resources, or there may be some breakdown in the flow of information from one team to the next. Whatever it is, the director should identify the problem and take steps to correct it, even bringing the problem to the attention of the executive leadership team if necessary.

Speaking of information, the TQM director helps interpret the data generated by various teams. The director is responsible for communicating progress and results to other teams and to the whole organization and its external stakeholders.

Finally, the director leads the executive leadership team through strategic planning for improvement, making sure quality isn't being done just for quality's sake, but for solid business reasons.

TQM Support Staff

The roles of the support staff are relatively easy to describe. They break down into two categories.

Responsibilities of TQM Support Staff

- Develop, implement, and manage the following TQM support processes:

—Team facilitation
—Communications
—Reward and recognition
—Recordkeeping and archiving
—Team empowerment
• Develop, implement, and manage the training process to include training needed by teams and facilitators.

Rather than detailing these self-explanatory activities, let's concentrate on a crucial and frequently misunderstood role.

Facilitators

In a TQM environment filled with newly formed teams, coaching is necessary, and facilitators make the best coaches. The team process is going to be foreign to many employees, and facilitators enable them to make the adjustment through the following activities.

Responsibilities of Facilitators

• Team start-up and initial training
• Facilitation/process management for key team meetings
• Team training on tools, methods, and project planning
• Team support—process consulting and troubleshooting

Helping teams learn to work together from the very beginning of the process is an essential task for facilitators. Later on, teams may find that they can function well on their own. But at the start, most teams need to learn how to negotiate a charter with their sponsor, for instance. We've found the executive leadership team, in particular, greatly benefits from a full-time facilitator. Because this team's time is so precious, anything that can be done to maximize the value the team delivers is important. A good facilitator can save other team members time, nudging them toward decisions and taking over relatively minor tasks from key members.

Facilitators help the team work out its training plan. In this capacity, they have access to a wide variety of quality improvement tools, and they can recommend certain tools and bring them in when a team seems to need them. It may be that the team requires instruction on what a good project plan looks like or how to use Pareto charts to analyze improvement opportunities. The facilitator may personally provide the training or bring in other resources.

Facilitators can also help the team get unstuck or back on the right track. By observing team meetings, a facilitator can identify the reason no progress is being made (people are defending their functional turf, for example) and step in and coach the team back to a productive path.

By this point, you probably understand that not just anyone can fulfill the role of facilitator. To find the right person for that role, see if a candidate possesses these qualifications:

1. *Sensitive to the group process.* Facilitators are skilled at group dynamics and are able to help others reach conclusions and achieve consensus.

2. *Intellectually and emotionally secure.* Facilitators aren't easily bullied and don't bully others. They're not afraid of conflicts or the highly charged emotions (people crying, yelling) that can be part of team meetings.

3. *Disassociated from the team's "activity" and not subordinate to anyone on the team.* Facilitators will have difficulty maintaining objectivity if they have a vested interest in the outcome of the team's work (a sales process vice-president facilitating a sales process improvement team, for example). Similarly, facilitators with lower rank than team members can be intimidated.

4. *Able to focus on process rather than content.* Facilitators facilitate the process, not the actual improvement or any other objective of the team. Yet some people naturally get caught up in the content, drawn into the nitty-gritty details—whether material A is better than material B, whether sales technique C is better than sales technique D. Some people have the knack of distancing themselves from these details and focusing on helping the team reach consensus on A or B, C or D.

Facilitators Working With Other Role Players

The TQM support structure intersects with the TQM structure up and down the line. Most of these intersections require no explanation: Common sense tells you how the support staff might provide the resources to set up a new recordkeeping system appropriate for postimprovement use, for example. But the intersection between facilitators and other roles deserves a little discussion.

Facilitators frequently interact with process owners or team leaders (heads of nonprocess teams) and sponsors. People assuming these key roles must be on the same wavelength with regard to team meetings. If they're not, meetings are called in which the agenda is created spur-of-the-moment, the resources that should be available to the team at the meeting aren't there, and the decisions reached at the meeting aren't communicated to everyone who should be aware of them.

To avoid this disorganized, unplanned approach to improvements, the roles of sponsors, facilitators, and team leaders/process owners must be clarified. It's all too easy for roles to get confused during interactions, and for crucial assignments to be overlooked. Here are a few examples of role responsibilities that should be clarified:

- Will the team leader lead meetings and only bring the facilitator in for the tough ones?
- Is the sponsor going to attend every meeting or be there only at milestones or on request?
- Is the team leader responsible for the agenda, or should the facilitator also take responsibility?
- Should the facilitator write the minutes of the meeting, and should they be sent out only after the team leader approves them?

Teaching the Organization How to Support Itself

Many improvements fail because teams don't capitalize on the support infrastructure. Teams are sometimes unaware of what resources are available to them; they don't always understand that certain resources even exist.

We know of a company that is pushing hard into benchmarking. It sent its executive leadership team to do benchmarking at very high leadership levels. This was a continuing process, and two years after it started, the company realized that the data gathered were virtually useless because they had never been organized—they were scattered about in desk drawers, in computers, and in the heads of people who had left the organization. It was entirely possible that the organization could take a benchmarking trip to a company like Motorola, only to hear the Motorola representative tell them, "Hey, you guys were here two years ago; why are you back?"

This happened because the company didn't have a TQM support structure to collect and organize data and to make them easily accessible.

The support structure not only makes a wide variety of resources available to the team structure but educates the teams about those resources.

One of the resources is the roadmap cube described in this book. As a conceptual approach to implementing TQM, the roadmap is a tool that all teams can use, but that not all teams will understand initially. The TQM director, support staff, and facilitators can foster that understanding. They're the ones who should know the map backwards and forwards and who can help guide others in its use.

Chapter 12

The Passage Through the Paradigm Shift

By now, many of you may have realized that our discussion of TQM and process improvements has a larger context. Though we've focused on the specifics of improvement phases, organizational levels, and business architecture (the three aspects of the roadmap cube), you should understand that what we've described is part of an all-encompassing change management process.

Quality initiatives demand change. From the way you manage to the way you measure, your organization is going to evolve as you try to make improvements. You may evolve from a pyramid structure to a flattened one, from a few people with decision-making power to a fully empowered work force. One way or another, you have to manage the changes that come with this evolution.

Some companies try to manage these changes in isolation. They seize upon a change management theory and end up managing only one part of the process. They do a wonderful job helping the company move from a bureaucratic structure to a team structure, but their change management approach ignores process and infrastructure reengineering. As a result, employees are confused or even scared by the changes occurring all around them. Resistance is their natural response.

The roadmap helps you reduce that resistance to change. As you'll see in this chapter, it enables your organization and your people to anticipate, prepare for, and adjust to the evolving styles and structures.

Stages, Dimensions, and Magnitude of Change

If you take a long view of the change process, you'll see the four stages featured in Exhibit 12-1 and the correspondences to the roadmap. In the

Exhibit 12-1. Stages of change.

Stage 1	Stage 2	Stage 3	Stage 4
Getting Started	Targeted Improvement	Extension to All Processes	Continuous Improvement
Front Face of Cube Executive Level	Phases Face	Front Face All Levels	Complete Cube

Focus

first or "getting started" stage, the executive level begins mapping the organization using the front face of the cube. In the second stage, it proceeds to targeted improvements and moves through all four phases. In the third stage, improvements take place in all processes at all levels of the business. In the fourth stage, continuous improvement is a reality. The entire cube has been worked through; teams are deployed everywhere working to improve everything.

But all these changes should not be pictured as a straight line. This is a four-dimensional experience, as shown in Exhibit 12-2.

We'll talk in greater detail about these dimensions and how they evolve later in the chapter. For now, you can see the extremes between Stage 1 and Stage 4. Though the charts are self-explanatory, we should point out a few key factors in each change dimension.

• *Management style.* Before change takes place, this style is often ruled by circumstance: Managers take action in response to some problem. By Stage 4, the style is proactive: Managerial behavior includes providing the necessary skills and resources when individuals or teams need them.

• *Measurement.* Traditional measurements are financially based and cannot offer a true reading of how processes are performing. There may be other measures for marketing or engineering, but they're not connected to one another or back to overall business measures. In addition, numerous informal or implied measures exist, embodied in statements such as, "We all know that what the boss is really looking for is. . . ." Such measures are difficult if not impossible to satisfy.

The evolution here is toward high-level measures that deal with all business drivers, not just financial ones. The measures are linked to process measures, so we can determine how a process improvement (or the lack thereof) contributes to overall business performance. These measures exist on all organizational levels, so even assembly-line workers can clearly relate the tasks they perform to business performance.

• *Structure.* The vertical to horizontal shift is easy to grasp. We should emphasize, however, that one of the most significant changes is the movement from a rigid bureaucracy to flexible teams. The ability to adjust quickly to new business circumstances will be essential.

• *Empowerment.* We're moving from the most important decisions being made at the top of the old organizational chart to teams able to make decisions at their own levels. Instead of the yo-yo process of

Exhibit 12-2. Dimensions of change.

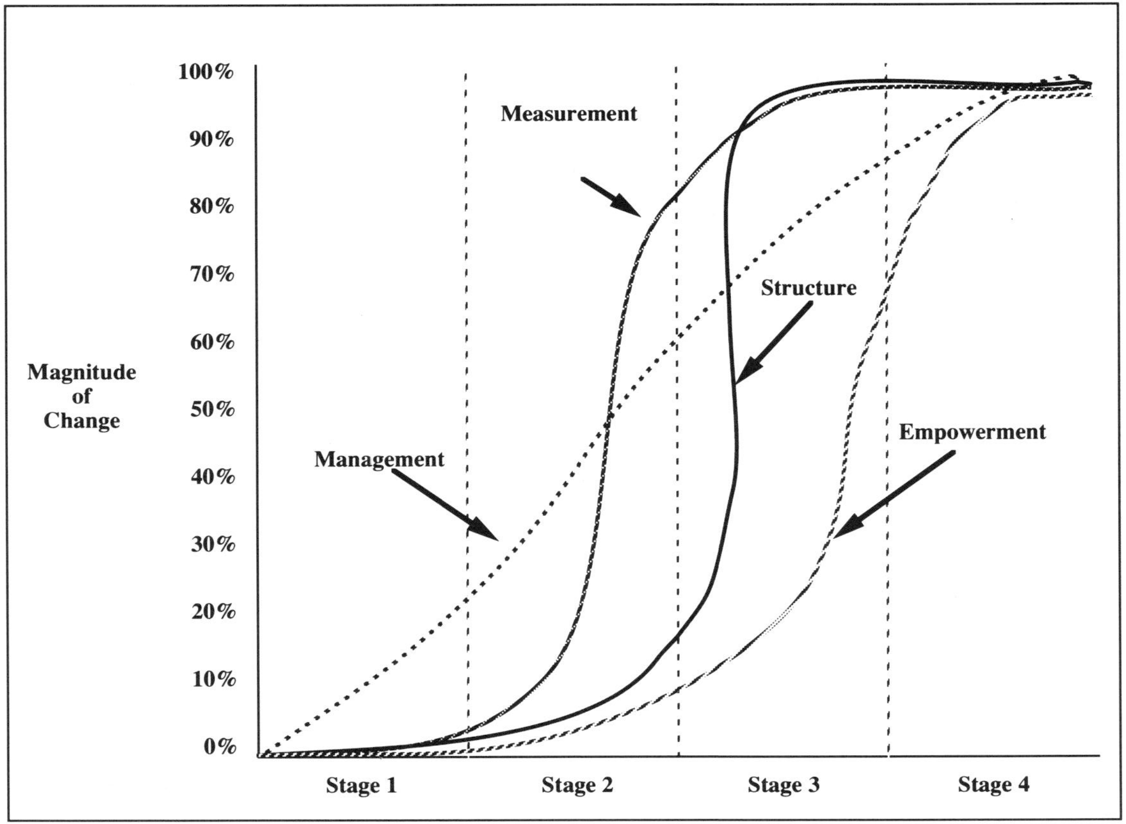

decision making, where decisions are passed up through one department, then down to another department, up through that department,
then down again, we'll see individuals and teams deciding quickly and
appropriately across departmental lines.

Finally, don't expect all this change to occur at the same pace in
each dimension.

From Exhibit 12-3, you can see that management starts changing
before the other dimensions in Stage 1, that the measurement system
changes very quickly between Stages 2 and 3, that structural changes
generally occur in Stage 3 when you deploy team structure, and that
empowerment is a consequence of changes in the other dimensions.

Though Exhibit 12-3 may not show it clearly, each change dimension interacts with the others. Which dimension leads change during an
interaction depends on the stage. For instance, management tends to
lead change when first interacting with measurements between Stages
2 and 3.

Now let's take a closer look at how your organization is likely to
evolve as you improve.

Measurement Evolution

The first big change involves creating a business measurement hierarchy
that reflects more than the financials and that links with processes.

But the paper measurement hierarchy has to evolve into a real,
functional system. The tasks of collecting data, assembling them into a
database, and issuing reports based on the new system are necessary if
you want to achieve real change.

The next big step occurs when your organization actually starts
using the measurement system and the data it generates for improvement planning and projects, problem solving, and decision making.

The change that signifies that you've arrived occurs when your
measurement system is fully institutionalized. This is when the ideal of
"management by fact" becomes reality. From the executive level to
hourly workers, everyone is plugged into a fully integrated set of
business measures.

Structural Evolution

Major change starts when the TQM team structure is overlaid on the
existing organization and you go after targets of improvement opportu-

Exhibit 12-3. Magnitude of changes.

Measurement Evolution	Structural Evolution	Empowerment Evolution	Management Evolution
Creating the measurement hierarchy	Beginning TQM team structure overlaid on the existing organization	Establishing the empowerment process by chartering and empowering the first targeted improvement teams	Executives learning what changes in role, style and behavior will be required
Measurements are linked to processes and measurement systems put in place	Team structure expanded to cover all processes at all levels	More teams empowered to cover more processes and there is deployment of empowerment down to working level teams (breadth and depth increase)	Transformation begins through a combination of education, learning by doing, feedback and coaching from facilitators, reward and recognition
The organization begins using measurement data for all problem solving /decision making/ improvement planning and projects	Redefining the underlying organization structure including delayering and horizontal process-focused structures linked to other structures that foster functional expertise	Fundamental decision processes are reshaped with redefined limits and roles at all levels	Managers throughout the organization have gotten the message and are working to make the changes. Selection of managers now includes screening for appropriate style and approach.
Measurement fully institutionalized and fully integrated top to bottom and across all processes	Flexible, flat, team-oriented organization capable of fast response to changing conditions and oriented to continuous improvement	Decisions being made appropriately at the lowest possible level with full support by management	Executives and managers function as leaders, enablers, coaches, integrators, and roadblock removers. Higher levels in the organization focus on strategies and change related issues, little on operational matter.

nity. You're not changing the existing organization; you're simply dropping the structural agent of change on top of it.

Next, you expand the TQM team structure to all processes and levels.

Third, you're ready to redefine the existing organizational structure, destratifying, creating process-focused structures, and linking the structures together. The overlaid TQM structure from the first major change gradually and naturally becomes the dominant structure as the old one fades away like the brittle, decaying thing that it is.

Your structure has fully evolved when it's flexible, flat, and process-oriented, and features interlaced team structures. If it's oriented to continuous improvement and able to adapt quickly to changing conditions, you're there.

Empowerment Evolution

Empowerment of both individuals and teams begins with chartering the first targeted improvement team. Empowerment is limited to relatively few employees and teams at the start.

Later in the process, more teams involved with more processes are empowered, and empowerment is now deployed down to working-level teams.

You've evolved further when the fundamental decision-making process in your organization has been redefined. Now everyone and every team understands what it's empowered to do (and not to do); limits and roles are clearly communicated and supported by management.

At the most advanced evolutionary point, decisions are being made at the lowest possible level, and the process is supported by all areas of the organization, including the reward and recognition system.

Management Evolution

The start of the evolution is a learning process: Executives are educated (and trained) about required changes in role, style, and behavior.

The actual transformation takes place through a variety of actions, from learning by doing (setting up a team) to feedback and coaching from facilitators. Over time, executives learn to reshape their behavior to fit the new paradigm, and a changed reward and recognition system encourages this reshaping.

The evolution is further along when managers throughout the organization "get the message." They're working to make the necessary behavioral changes, and the company has progressed far enough that the selection process for new managers includes screening for appropriate behavior and style.

At the fully evolved point, executives function as leaders, enablers, coaches, integrators, and roadblock removers. The higher-level executives have almost totally extricated themselves from operational matters and are focused on strategy and on organizational capability and effectiveness.

The Roadmap and Change

No doubt you have seen many books and articles about change management or heard about the consultants who specialize in this area. Although there's nothing wrong with any of these things, they aren't the total solution to managing the issues raised by change.

Each book or consultant specializes in one of the four change dimensions, teaching, for example, how to implement empowerment strategies or how to create a new organizational structure. So when you practice what one of them preaches, your focus is one-dimensional. As you try to cope with change, you stall out.

The problem, of course, is that the four change dimensions are inextricably linked. If you give your complete and undivided attention to empowerment, you'll never reach your empowerment goals because you've failed to do anything about measurement, structure, or management. You may want to evolve to the point where decisions are made at the lowest possible level, but you can't get there because you've neglected to manage and evolve executive behaviors.

The roadmap ensures that nothing is neglected. The cube contains all the elements of the four change dimensions. If you use the cube in your mapping, you will have to address each dimension.

Just as important, the roadmap allows you to address change systematically and logically, rather than in isolation. Without a systems structure like the roadmap, organizations seize upon a change management approach and try to implement it. Management is shuttled to training sessions in which it learns new management techniques. As you might expect, managers often scoff at and resist those techniques, or they embrace them and charge ahead with potential solutions. To most people, the new approach seems to have come out of the blue.

The roadmap offers context. It provides an organizing, integrating, systems framework into which the many excellent change, organizational, and improvement strategies can be fitted. As you'll recall from Exhibit 12-1, change progresses in stages that correspond to aspects of the cube. There are reference points that make change a little less scary. Changes in structure, such as team formation, and changes in measurement systems (from financial-based to overall business measures) are addressed and predicted by the roadmap.

The natural evolution of the four change dimensions discussed here is tolerated better by employees when they know what's coming. If you can familiarize your people with this evolutionary process, use the roadmap to manage the changes that occur, and integrate the best ideas of the gurus and the best practices of other companies, you'll arrive at TQM faster, more cheaply, and more effectively than your competitors.

Chapter 13

Reality Check: Can We Really Do This With Our Business?

Perhaps you're thinking that as good as the roadmap sounds, you're never going to be able to put it to use in your organization. It would require nothing less than a transformation of the entire business. Though you might agree that such a transformation is necessary or desirable, you can't afford to stop doing business while you're changing the business. Who is going to produce the products and services while you're tinkering with processes?

As much as we'd like to give you an easy answer to that question, the only true answer is that quality isn't easy. You can't put the business on hold while you're figuring out the roadmap.

But the roadmap can help you reach the new paradigm we discussed in Chapter 12 faster, better, and more cheaply. That doesn't make improvement easy, but it does make it easier. What also makes it easier is facing some hard truths about what the path to high performance will be like.

Bumps in the Road

1. *You can't stop running the business while you start your improvement efforts.* We've already mentioned this first hard truth. It would be nice if that were possible, since it would give you the time and perspective necessary to reinvent the company. But the reality is that you have to start with an almost schizophrenic mindset: While part of you is moving the business toward the new paradigm, another part of you is running the business under the old paradigm. By acknowledging that you'll have these two conflicting responsibilities initially, you're able to reconcile them somewhat.

2. *In the short term, you'll have to invest more time and money than you'll get back.* For companies with overworked executives and tight budgets, that's an unattractive prospect. During those first few months, and perhaps for an even longer period, you must accept that your return won't appear on the balance sheets.

3. *You may be betting the company and top managers' careers.* This is especially true if you attack quality issues with speed and aggressiveness. Some organizations can't wait for the long-term return on their investment in quality; other times, boards of directors are too impatient for results. You may be working with or for someone who thinks TQM is a bunch of esoteric nonsense, and if you don't deliver results, you and your quality nonsense may be on the street. Whatever the case, you should accept that for top management as well as the organization, there is risk.

4. *Short-term fear and upheaval may occur.* TQM means change, dismantling the status quo, risk, and many other things that terrify some people. For organizations under significant financial pressure, the fear becomes palpable. For them, TQM may be the final roll of the dice with everything riding on that roll. Frayed nerves, nervous stomachs, and disorganization may be prevalent in early stages. From a purely personal standpoint, employees worry about where they will fit into the new system and wonder where these improvements will take them.

5. *Deintegration is likely at the start.* This is the ironic result of the improvement process: If you improve one thing, another will be thrown out of synch. Few organizations can afford to improve every process at once to ensure harmonious integration; it's often a one-process-at-a-time chronology. Yet none of this matters when deintegration rears its ugly head. More than any other truth, this one is difficult to swallow. Before you embark on your quality effort, everything is integrated. Sales and manufacturing and distribution and order entry all have an acceptable system for interacting, with relatively few glitches. That system may not be particularly effective or efficient, but it does work. When you fix a process and make it more efficient and effective, this creates a disconnect with other processes. Your new order entry system relays orders through the system faster than ever before, but your MIS system doesn't communicate the right information about the orders to the right people. The disconnect has everyone pulling their hair out—orders are lost and forms can't be filled out properly.

It's at this point that many organizations throw up their hands in bewilderment and frustration. They can't continue on their quality journey because of the disconnect, but they can't go back to the way things were because they've invested too much in the TQM effort. Like someone stuck in the middle of a raging river, they can go back to the safety of the shore they came from or cross over to the safety of the other side, but in the meantime, the river rages on.

All these hard truths remind us of another analogy used by one of our clients, who compared the initial months of improvements to "changing the tires on a moving truck." Yes, it's difficult. But it can be done if you have the proper help to do it.

Putting On Good Tires, Minimizing the Risks

With all that said, let us add that the hard truths don't have to turn into impenetrable roadblocks. In fact, there are a number of ways to make those truths more palatable and the risk more acceptable. Here's how.

• *Follow the roadmap.* The fear, the upheaval, the deintegration between processes—all can be lessened by using the roadmap. You can anticipate and plan for the deintegration; Phase 4 of the roadmap keeps reminding you to deal with integration issues. The systematic approach to improvements offered by the roadmap lessens the uncertainty and chaos; it suggests a logical, viable method of making improvements. The project management methodology and downward deployment of strategic goals minimize the financial risks—you're initially targeting improvement opportunities that will give your business what it needs most. If you determine that your business desperately needs an infusion of revenue, your improvements will be tailored to that goal. Most important of all, the roadmap's front face allows you to see your business in a connected, holistic perspective. When you see the connections, you're less likely to miss some crucial step or overlook an important resource.

• *Create a vision.* People become dispirited when they're not sure where the quality effort is taking them. Employees want to know what's in it for them if they do what management wants. If the executive leadership team can create a vision of the future for employees, it reassures them by shining a light on the road ahead. When a pilot test fails or when middle managers find themselves struggling with new roles, people need a sense that the problems and struggles are worth it. When employees can envision a better, more productive organization in the future, it can justify their present difficulties. A good analogy is the wagon trains that crossed the country to California. The vision of sun, plentiful land, and ocean kept everyone pulling together through a long, arduous journey.

• *Set tough goals.* Because the journey is hard, you can't be satisfied with moderate goals. Unless you are willing to wait a long time or risk getting bogged down, keep your goals tough. Motorola, for instance, has set the very exacting standard of six sigma for defects per million; General Electric has declared that if a product line isn't number one or two in its market, the line will be sold off. At the same time, however, don't set impossible goals—zero defects, for instance, is statistically unrealistic in a world of variability and will simply frustrate people.

• *Choose the right people.* More specifically, the executive leadership team should be sure to include the following three types of people on the teams:

Preacher:	The evangelical leader who espouses the quality religion with fervor and who gets everyone inspired and moving
Planner:	The organizer who understands the roadmap and has experience in moving an organization systematically and sequentially through improvements
Tools purveyor:	Someone who understands, has access to, and can provide the resources needed, from statistical analysis to specific types of training

This doesn't mean you need just three people. You may need scores of planners, a few preachers, and many tools purveyors. It all depends on your organization and its particular situation.

The biggest mistake organizations make here is relying on one person for everything. We've seen a number of companies that have hired one consultant and expected that consultant to be a jack of all quality trades. Most consultants specialize in one of the above three areas, and to expect them to be competent in the others makes no sense. Firms hire a top quality guru hoping for a turnkey quality operation, but what he or she really provides is religion, as is appropriate for a preacher role only.

• *Manage the pace.* Finding the perfect speed for improvements is a challenge. Go too fast and you'll burn out; go too slow and you'll stall. The executive leadership team must exert enough pressure to maintain visible movement toward improvement goals without allowing the movement to spin out of control. A string of impossible deadlines will burn anyone out, and making no progress toward a goal paralyzes initiative.

Managing the pace also means watching for stragglers. If one team is 12 months ahead of another, integration is impossible. If you see a team lagging too far behind, you have to provide that team with the resources and incentives necessary to catch up, or at least stay close.

Finally, manage the pace with encouragement. Literal and figurative pats on the back are crucial when teams are pushing hard toward difficult objectives. When top managers are visibly involved as team members, everyone else works harder—management is backing up its words about quality with actions. Encouragement and participation shouldn't come just from the CEO, but from every member of the executive leadership team and from leaders everywhere in the organization.

Leap of Faith

To paraphrase an old military saying, there are no atheists in TQM foxholes. You need a little blind faith to get you through some rough times. That's not always easy. Because the TQM movement is relatively young, you can't pore over scores of case histories from the Harvard Business School and reassure yourself that what you're trying has been successfully done by others. Even the Baldrige Award winners and other companies with quality success stories are not perfect models; they are all relative neophytes, despite their accomplishments. Stories abound about companies that have invested in TQM and stalled. Most organizations still have a long way to go before they reach TQM.

So how do you know it exists? Empirically, you don't know. But even a casual observer of the gains a systematic improvement approach has allowed companies like Motorola, GE, Corning, Federal Express, Ford, and TRW (not to mention the Japanese) to make should convince you that the theory is sound. If this quality approach has yielded significant benefits in its initial stages, the benefits should be even greater when these companies are much further down the TQM road.

Faith will help guard against impatience, a potential enemy of the improvement process. Some organizations are so anxious to make improvements and so frustrated when they don't progress quickly enough that they push their people harder than they should. But when they go too fast, not only do their people burn out, but they skip crucial steps, and this frequently comes back to haunt them in the integration phase.

Faith also comes harder for companies in the middle of the road. By "in the middle," we mean companies that are neither in the express lane, flush with success and huge cash resources, nor on the shoulder, headed for the ditch and teetering on the edge of financial disaster. The former has the luxury of faith: Even if improvement efforts don't yield results initially, the company has a financial cushion it can fall back on. The latter can take a damned-if-we-do, damned-if-we-don't attitude: It really has nothing to lose by trying it.

If you're in between those two extremes (as most organizations are), you will be vulnerable to the impatience, cynicism, and skepticism that has struck other companies. To lessen your vulnerability, rely on the roadmap. One of the most faith-inspiring aspects of the map is the way it helps you focus on the right improvement targets first. The targeting power of the map enables you to do the things that are most crucial to the business. When an improvement project delivers measurable results, everyone's faith in TQM is enhanced.

Finally, and most important, there is no substitute for strong, committed leadership. Every organization that has had major success with its quality effort has enjoyed such leadership. The leap of faith in quality must first be made at the top of the organization. Only then will others follow and the commitment to TQM spread organizationwide.

Conclusion: On the Road Again

If you've gained nothing more than a fresh perspective from reading this book, then we believe the book should have value for you. Though we hope you've gained much more, we've found that organizations make great strides toward business goals when they look at quality from a targeted, connected, and holistic perspective. At its core, the roadmap is a framework that allows you to view your quality effort in new and enlightening ways.

Throughout this book, we've discussed the ins and outs of that framework, offering as much information as possible to help your organization overcome roadblocks and reach quality-related goals. Certainly you can refer to relevant chapters if you get stuck or if you're uncertain what to do next. But in addition to the information contained in the body of the book, we thought it might be worthwhile to compile a list of ten questions that you can refer to, a checklist of sorts to be certain that you're on course.

1. *Are you doing quality for quality's sake or for the business's sake?* Some organizations are so eager to jump on the quality bandwagon that they lose sight of where it's taking the business. These organizations fail to make clear connections between their improvements and their strategic business goals. Quality can be terribly expensive, especially if you haven't nailed down exactly what you want a quality program to achieve. Tom Gilbert, the human performance technology theorist, wrote a book declaring, "Behavior second, results first." In other words, judge quality in terms of the results you're getting. Don't assume the program is a success just because an isolated improvement was successful. Always ask how that improvement contributed to larger company objectives.

2. *Has your quality effort significantly changed the way you run your business, from selection and reward systems to executive behavior?* If it hasn't, something is wrong. TQM is not cosmetic; it gets below the surface and alters the status quo. If nothing much changes, you haven't made much progress toward TQM. One litmus test is to examine your "before" and "after" deployment of resources: They should be dramatically different. Similarly, your employees should be rewarded for new types of behavior—taking risks and failing versus playing it close to the vest and marginally succeeding. A closer-to-home example may be an analysis of how top executives are spending their time. Ideally, they'll be spending a great deal of time together as a team, assessing the business and targeting improvements. If they're still doing the same old things—dwelling on operational results and troubleshooting current issues—the quality effort has bogged down.

3. *Are your quality efforts targeted or shotgun?* The shotgun approach can be defined as setting up as many teams as possible to work on improvements. This is like betting on every number on the roulette wheel to guarantee a winner. It doesn't work in gambling, and it doesn't work in quality. From the very start, focus on the improvements that will help your business the most.

4. *Is there a system in place to integrate the hundreds of changes and improvements that will take place?* Organizations think they've struck quality gold when an improvement pays off in a big way. They're convinced they have the secret to quality. What they really have is the possibility that one good result will trigger ten bad ones. We've seen scores of companies make successful improvements, only to find that those improvements caused disconnects with other processes, resulting in chaos. Improvements that take place in isolation are symptomatic of the wrong approach to quality. Examine whether you've really mapped out your business using the front face of the roadmap—if you've accounted for and made connections among all the processes, stakeholder requirements, and infrastructure elements.

5. *When you map out your quality effort, can you see it unfolding over a period of weeks, months, or years?* If you do it right, you can see far into the future. Many organizations find they can actually sequence their improvement targets, starting with the most important and proceeding down the road for years until a state of continuous improvement and total quality is achieved. This ability to line up improvement targets far down the line is more important than it may initially seem. It provides executive leadership with an understanding of where the quality effort is going and what specific benefits can be expected, reassuring doubters

and cynics who are skeptical about where all the investments in improvements are taking the organization.

6. *Are you committed to making an investment in quality?* Some people believe that quality is free—or at least, that it should be free. In reality, most companies have to make a substantial initial investment. If they've hit the big improvement targets first, they quickly break even, and only then does quality become free. Forecasting your quality investment is essential. If management is shocked to find that it has to spend a lot of money on quality or if it finds it lacks the necessary resources in mid-journey, the quality effort can stall.

7. *Are you in control of your improvements?* You may know how much you're investing, but you may not know what your return on investment is. Improvements are complicated, and quality cannot be made simple. We've emphasized that one improvement can have repercussions throughout the organization, and that if you aren't aware of and haven't planned for or adjusted to those repercussions, you'll encounter difficulties. Control means using the roadmap to approach improvements in a targeted, prioritized, comprehensive manner.

8. *How do your employees feel about the quality effort?* If they hate even the mention of the "Q" word, then you have a big problem. Morale-destroying downsizing and other moves sometimes accompany quality initiatives. While downsizing may be necessary, it should be handled in such a way that the quality movement isn't turned into a villain. Just as bad is when your people perceive that they're being punished for finding efficiencies—they help you make an improvement, and it seems to cost them their jobs or their promotions. It's also possible that although your employees don't hate quality, they're cynical about it. Part of the cynicism stems from nonapplied training—employees receive intensive training in things like statistical process control, but are never given a chance to use it. There are scores of examples of management talking one way about quality but acting another.

9. *How do your other stakeholders feel about your quality efforts?* Unless the major stakeholders, from the board of directors to suppliers to customers, have bought in to quality and are committed to it, you're going to experience roadblocks. One of the most insidious problems is a board that gives tacit approval to quality efforts, only to balk when push comes to shove—additional resources are needed, an improvement doesn't pan out, pressure for short-term results comes from the investment community. It's also very easy to abuse stakeholders while making improvements—to lean too hard on suppliers for price reduc-

tions, for instance. You need to balance all your stakeholders' requirements, not just work to satisfy one particular stakeholder.

10. *Is a common language being spoken?* As a word, quality has so many meanings that it's virtually meaningless. The way Crosby talks about quality is somewhat different from the way Deming talks about it. Each day seems to bring a new quality tool, concept, or award. If members of your executive leadership team subscribe to different quality gurus, for example, they may not be able to talk the same language. Not only are the concepts different, the jargon is also different. Integration of various improvements is critical, and the lack of a common language can frustrate that integration. The roadmap provides a framework for a common language and will accommodate most of the well-known quality concepts. If you have strategically deployed quality as the roadmap recommends, you will also deploy a common language and philosophy.

Where Do We Go From Here?

As important as it is to keep these ten questions in mind, they don't tell you what to do when you finish this book. Many organizations are wondering what to do—what to do when their quality effort stalls, when their process improvements cause disconnects with other processes, when they achieve improvement goals but fall short of business ones. Ideally, we would be able to tell you the right steps to take (and the wrong ones to avoid) at every crossroads you come to on the way to TQM.

Realistically, however, the directions for one company are inappropriate for another. What to do is a function of your particular situation and business strategy—a market-leading company with tremendous cash assets will require one set of directions, a market challenger with limited cash but superior technological assets a different one.

Thus, the roadmap. We've designed it for every type of organization, no matter what your situation might be. Though it doesn't tell you exactly what to do, it does guide you toward a path that is viable for your company. It does so by letting you assess, test, deploy, and integrate your improvements in a more holistic, connected way than you've probably ever considered before. Within a quality context, the roadmap is revelatory; it reveals the hidden linkages, business drivers, and other factors that can make or break your quality effort.

To begin using it, you don't have to do anything more than assemble an executive leadership team and begin mapping your organization as suggested by the front face of the roadmap cube. As you begin detailing, breaking down, and connecting all the processes, business drivers, and infrastructure resources, you'll realize that you're creating a new architecture for your business—an architecture that is compatible with TQM.

This isn't brain surgery. Contrary to what many people believe, you don't have to hire scores of outside experts to help you with your quality program. Most of the resources you'll need are inside your organization. The roadmap is designed to help you tap those resources and use them to achieve the strategic goals of the business—and not just achieve them, but do so faster, more cheaply, and better.

Index